ity
ng

Corporate Facility Planning

An Inside View for Designers and Managers

Stephen Binder

McGraw-Hill Book Company

New York   St. Louis   San Francisco   Auckland   Bogotá
Caracas   Colorado Springs   Hamburg   Lisbon
London   Madrid   Mexico   Milan   Montreal
New Delhi   Oklahoma City   Panama   Paris
San Juan   São Paulo   Singapore
Sydney   Tokyo   Toronto

Library of Congress Cataloging-in-Publication Data

Binder, Stephen.
  Corporate facility planning : an inside view for designers and
managers / Stephen Binder.

     p.   cm.
  Includes index.
  ISBN 0-07-005289-1
  1. Facility management.   I. Title.
TS177.B56 1989
658.2—dc19   88-23489
                                                      CIP

  34567890   DOC/DOC   9543210

ISBN 0-07-005289-1

*The editors for this book were Joel E. Stein and Nancy Young, the
designer was Naomi Auerbach, and the production supervisor was
Suzanne W. Babeuf. It was set in Century Schoolbook. It was composed
by the McGraw-Hill Book Company, Professional & Reference Division
composition unit.*

Printed and bound by R. R. Donnelley & Sons Company.

*For more information about other McGraw-Hill materials,
call 1-800-2-MCGRAW in the United States. In other
countries, call your nearest McGraw-Hill office.*

DEDICATION

To Bonnie, Kasi, Keith, Lon—
You are my soul and inspiration.

And, in fond memory of my Dad, Harry Binder,
who passed away while I was writing this book.

Contents

Preface

fa.cil.i.ty man.age.ment, n.

*The practice of coordinating the physical
workplace with the people and work of the
organization; integrates the principles of
business administration, architecture, and
the behavioral and engineering sciences.*

Library of Congress, 1985.

"Facility Management" is a term that came into use in 1979. The profession has been around since the first organization needed an individual to make a small renovation. No one knows when this occurred.

Facility management as a field incorporates many diverse functions:

Master space planning

Space inventory

Space and furniture standards setting

Project management (administration and implementation)

Programming requirements

Financial control (budgeting and forecasting)

Scheduling

Layout and design

Purchasing (furniture and construction items)

Construction management

Ongoing maintenance management

In organizations, the business plan should be the driving force for a successful facilities plan. It is unfortunate when a business manager has to rely on the facility manager's information as the sole basis of that business plan.

The facility management function exists in an organization to contribute to the bottom line profitability of each business unit through increased efficiency and reduced costs in operations, space rental, and ongoing fixed costs.

Corporate project/facilities management requires special abilities beyond the basic understanding of the multifunctions listed earlier. Management of the facility process is essential for one's initial success, continued success, and continuous employment in the field. The facility manager must deal with corporate politics and fiscal restraints while managing various professional disciplines to accomplish assigned project tasks.

This book follows the roles, practices, and realities of a facility manager throughout the life cycle of a project. *Corporate Facility Planning* deals with a logical, practical, actually tested, successful methodology of managing and coping with the corporate facilities management functions. It is unique in that I have been in the corporate environment over 21 years and as far as I know this is the first book written from within the corporation.

Corporate Facility Planning is intended as a guide for:

The already successful facility manager who needs reassurance that the daily "unbelievably" stressful job situations are, in fact, routine.

The facility manager who has been unsuccessful or has been overtaken by corporate bureaucracy and needs a quick refresher course in survival.

The external architectural designer, interior designer, and other consultants who are all involved with facility managers but do not quite understand what drives this *new* breed of professional.

The multitude of vendors selling or marketing design, engineering, furniture, equipment, or construction resources who also must contend with this "in-house" professional.

The individuals who are within the corporation and were planning a career in facility management—until they read what their work load would be.

The students currently enrolled in academic courses that lead to a degree and career in facilities management. This book serves as an encouragement to stay with it.

Keeping a slight bent toward a sense of humor has allowed me to get this far. It is highly recommended that one keeps a sane view of events. Do not take yourself or corporate criticism too seriously; otherwise you will be looking down on your next project from the field office in the sky!

The professional facility manager is only as good as the last successful project. *Sic transit gloria mundi.* How quickly fame fades.

Corporate Facility Planning is divided into three parts.

First stage: Establishing the basics

This part includes discussions, "how to" advice, and examples in space planning, space inventory, stacking, standards, and the project management approach.

Second stage: Applying the basics to the facility management process

This part includes discussions, "how to" advice, and examples to use during the project feasibility phase, interior design phase, purchasing phase, contract management phase, and construction management phase.

Third stage: Applying the basics to the fourth dimension of time

This part includes lessons that the facility manager should have learned on the job over time. Those new in the field will learn from those of us who had no predecessors. Discussions include the role of the facility manager dealing with facilities that are both "dumb" and "smart" and perceptions of a marketed facility manager.

All the views expressed herein are definitely those from the corporate viewpoint. What do those on the other side of the fence think about dealing with the facility manager throughout the project life? I didn't know for sure, so I asked them. Throughout the text are "The Words of Others," wherein professionals were asked to give their thoughts and opinions (a chance to gain or lose clients) in the context of the appropriate section. These professionals' thoughts are equally important for the facility manager to gain a better understanding of "where consultants are coming from" since they must be utilized for the success of the project. These professionals have helped facility managers look good within their corporations somewhere, sometime. In general, a consultant is brought on as an extension of the facility manager's team. The corporation is the winner when the team is successful.

In my years of giving speeches, writing articles, giving seminars, and living life each day in the office, I have tried to maintain a sense of humor about the very happenings of the position of facility manager. I have tried to maintain some of the humor, where appropriate, in this book.

To conclude this introduction, here is a question for those familiar with musical oldies: What was the first record album dedicated to the facility manager?

Here are some clues:

1. The album was an instant hit and went to Number 1 upon release.

2. The album was released a little over 20 years ago.

3. The album was by the Beatles.

4. It was a theme album that changed music after it was released.

A good guess if you thought *A Hard Day's Night*, but not correct. The answer is *Sgt. Pepper's Lonely Hearts Club Band!*

Let's review the reasons for the album's pertinence to the facility manager.

1. The facility manager's constant search for assistance is captured in "A Little Help from My Friends."

2. The answer the facility manager gives when management asks, "How's it going?" is

   I'm doing the best I can,
   I've got to admit it's "Getting Better."

3. The facility manager's duties as maintenance manager were covered in "Fixing a Hole (where the rain gets in)" and in "When I'm Sixty-Four": "I could be handy mending a fuse when your lights have gone."

4. Space shortages due to the user group's inaccurate forecast are covered in the opening lines from the song "Within You, Without You":

   We were talking about the space between us all
   And the people who hide themselves behind a wall of
   illusion
   Never glimpse the truth, then it's far too late.

5. The constant search for the user to inform the facility manager in advance of their exact needs also appears in the song "When I'm Sixty-Four":

   Send me a postcard, drop me a line
   Stating point of view
   Indicate precisely what you mean to say.

6. The facility manager's employment status is under question when the move-in is running behind schedule. This is covered in "Good Morning, Good Morning":

   Everybody knows there's nothing doing
   Everything is closed it's like a ruin
   Everyone you see is half asleep
   And you're on your own you're in the street.

7. The end user's constant complaint about the facility manager's constantly enforcing standards is covered in "Getting Better":

   You're holding me down, turning me round
   Filling me up with your rules.

8. The title itself, *Sgt. Pepper's Lonely Hearts Club Band*, is apt enough.

The facility manager may not have any friends or allies within the corporation.

Why can't users communicate precisely what they need?

How do we forecast for maintenance needs?

How do we deal with the user who is not giving us that glimpse of truth for space needs?

How does the facility manager get help from within the corporation?

All of these references are reviewed within this book. Helpful hints that have proven successful on how to overcome these deficits are included.

I hope the information provided will allow facility managers to be more professional and expert, as the Beatles sang in "A Day in the Life," for *having read the book*.

Stephen Binder

Acknowledgments

In October 1987 I celebrated my twenty-first anniversary of working at Citibank, N.A. I don't care to count the number of different people I worked for during those years. However, special thanks go to my division head since September 1972, Henry (Hal) Deford, III. Under Hal, I was given the opportunity to produce the first 5-year corporate master space plan developed by a Citibank in-house employee. I was allowed to present this plan to senior management, and I wasn't even a corporate officer at the time. (Those of you in corporations can appreciate the significance of this.) I still retain the title of corporate space planner through the present, and have added many other responsibilities along the way. Hal has supported my growth in the profession and my growth at Citibank.

Am I doing a terrific job? Or is it that no one else in the company wants the job?

I extend thanks to my staff of a dozen project managers, whom I consider my professional colleagues. They have helped to make me successful by being so talented and following the processes outlined in the book. I have had one of the lowest turnover rates of any manager in the company. Most of my staff have been with me since 1976. Are they still with me because I am a good supervisor? Or am I paying them too much?

Also thanks to "The Words of Others" authors for reading and responding to my call for a different viewpoint on their assigned topics. They provided excellent commentary, editing notes, and enthusiasm when I needed it. These people are all well known in the facilities field: Marshall A. Graham, Neville Lewis, Ralph Mancini, Ronald J. Goodrich, Theodore B. Stout, Robert C. Pew, Jerome Paul, Michael D. Tatum, and Anne Fallucchi. Special thanks to Floria V. Lasky, who is a terrific lawyer.

I owe the biggest thanks to my family. My wife, Bonnie, inspired me to write this book. She made me abandon the pen-and-paper approach from the very first day and just sit at our Apple II GS and *go*.

One goal of *Corporate Facility Planning* was to make sure that the terms were clear and understandable by all readers. Bonnie served as the perfect proofreader and editor because her business background is the design and manufacturer of men's and women's clothing! Bonnie had no real understanding of facilities management or any of its terminology.

To my daughter, Kasi, and my sons, Keith and Lon, thank you for letting me use the computer while you gave up *Star Blazer, Paintworks, Music Studio, Gold Rush*, and *Lode Runner*. The computer is yours until the next time.

Corporate Facility
Planning

First Stage:
Establishing
the Basics

Space:
The First Frontier

1.1 Introduction

The opening line from Star Trek *understated the value of space by calling it the final frontier. It is the* first *frontier.*

In certain states, possession is a certain percentage in divorce proceedings. In the corporate environment, possession of space is 100 percent, or *everything*. The facility manager is the business manager's best friend when space is available and is on the verge of unemployment when no space is to be found.

The World Book Dictionary defines space as "the unlimited room or place extending in all directions...." There are some interesting twists that occur during the facility manager's space planning assignment.

How much vacant space should be maintained?

- *Maintain unlimited vacant space.* Facility manager is not achieving corporate goals of profitably because vacant space costs money.

- *Always have a shortage of space.* Facility manager is not achieving corporate goals of properly planning for growth and change.

- *Maintain exactly the right amount of space vacant at all times.* Always achievable when the corporation grows as planned. The unplanned changes are the culprits. How the facility manager may capture accurate information on growth is discussed.

How is vacant space assigned?

- *Always satisfy space on a first-come basis.* This method always leads to departmental disputes for the same limited space. The second requester for the vacant space will undoubtedly have facts and figures to reflect business profits (the bottom-line mentality) as the reason for space assignment.

■ *Accumulate space requests for a while.* This method allows a fairer distribution of the limited vacant space. The facility manager assigns the space to the department with the "highest and best" need. This method puts the facility manager in a role that belongs to senior management. This method keeps the earlier requester from meeting business needs because of having to wait for a space assignment.

Role of the facility manager in planning

The facility manager must attempt to be absolutely neutral in evaluating space requests and in decision making. The space plan, done in advance and updated regularly, should be the living document for space assignments.

The basis for space decisions, when made, should take into consideration:

■ Sound thinking
■ Corporate goals and philosophy
■ Economics of the project and the times
■ Consideration for the master space plan

Master space plan

The master space plan comprises three generic types of space planning:

Type	Planning
Macro	
Facility term:	Long-range space plan
Business response:	"We can't be concerned that far into the future."
Micro	
Facility term:	Short-term planning
Business response:	"We will know better in two months. Come back then."
Daily	
Facility term:	Instant planning
Business response:	"If we wanted it tomorrow, we would have asked you tomorrow."

All three types interact and may cause changes to each other. A sound macroplan should have the least amount of changes because it has the long-range plans of the corporation as its foundation. If the long-range plans change, usually there is no impact on daily planning. It's possible to have changes to the microplan.

A change in the microplan may redirect daily planning efforts to the new plan. The microplan will also have an impact on the macroplan. Long-range plans rely on the validity of the microplan.

A change in the daily plan will have almost no impact on the macroplan owing to the time lag. However, it will directly change the corporation's microplan to accommodate any current changes.

Stacking

These plans are presented to senior management in a readable and understandable format. This is usually done via the stacking plan. The stacking plan presents the space planning recommendations in an orderly fashion. This is usually a building profile, with each floor clearly showing the occupants. A stacking plan is done for each time period of the master plan.

Inventory

When all planning and stacking have been accomplished, you must track all the information on corporate occupancy. This is done through a space inventory. The corporation's need to track departmental profit and loss through charges for space is called an allocation or charge-back system.

Summary

This chapter reviews space planning, stacking plans, and space inventory techniques. The one skill that is absolutely necessary for you is the ability to think in the fourth dimension of time. This simple concept is also discussed. The facility manager should never plan for today's corporate space solution without considering the impact on future business plans. The facility manager measures the impact in square footage while the corporation measures the impact in dollars.

1.2   Space Planning

Macroplan

The most difficult type of planning is the corporate space plan for an extended period of time. This type of planning is known as long-range planning, master space planning, or just macroplanning.

The plan frequently covers a significant time period in the corporate life and may be based on "real" data or data that has no business plan for support. Generally, the length of time is at least 5 years and could extend to 10 years. Unfortunately, much of the plan's form is based on information from business managers who may not be in the same job later in the space plan's life. Business managers may not be able to anticipate the future dynamics of their own business.

Microplan

The microplan covers a period of time of 1 to 4 years. This plan is required since you must submit financial forecasts of planned expenditures for the coming year(s). The facility manager normally plans a sequence of moves in the course of space planning. The completion of one relocation results in the renovation of the vacated area for the next unit. In turn, this move results in a third move in the series. Just a few significant moves results in a 2- to 3-year sequence. The facility manager utilizes the series of moves, in addition to other work assignments, to justify staffing needs to senior management.

Information gathered in microplanning tends to be far more accurate than in macroplanning. Business managers provide information that forecasts needs over a 2- to 24-month period. Moves scheduled later in the plan sequence are the most subject to change.

The facility manager always expects accurate information, without any fabrication, from the business manager. The facility manager always expects changes in this information over time. The business manager always plans for the best situation for the department while economic conditions may make the forecast too low, too high, or, in rare cases, exactly correct.

A move contrary to the long-range plan, but essential to resolve the microplan, may be subject to a review by senior management, who may disapprove the funding or change the long-range plan. The facility manager may recommend solutions.

Daily planning

There is absolutely no excuse for daily planning. Daily planning means that the business or facility manager did not plan for change properly. A review of the roots of daily planning through problem seeking reveals the following questions:

- Why can't the business managers inform the facility manager when ordering that new equipment?
- Why can't the business managers inform the facility manager,when

filling out the employee requisition, that there is no workstation for that employee?

- Why can't the business managers stick to their business plan after only 2 months?

- Why not inform the facility manager when the plans for the business change?

- Why don't the business managers communicate with the facility managers?

- *Communicating* means that two or more people are sending and receiving messages. Communication is a two-way street.

- Why must the facility manager wait to hear that new equipment is being ordered?

- Why must the facility manager wait to hear that a new employee has started working and the employee doesn't have a workstation?

- Why must the facility manager wait to hear about the change in the business plan?

- Why can't the facility manager communicate directly with the business manager?

The facility manager can and must communicate. Do not sit back and wait. Do not be reactive. You will never catch up with the changes.

The proactive state of the profession is to be an integral part of the everyday planning for the department. Business plans, changes, and staffing needs will be known in advance. Business managers welcome the support. When the ability to be close to the business manager is not available, you must be resourceful.

Business managers must have a main contact for changes. Business managers feel comfortable with one of their employees in this contact or coordinator role. This coordinator becomes your eyes and ears for changes. This departmental or user coordinator works for the business manager but reports on a matrix basis to the facility manager. The user coordinator becomes part of the project team. This concept is discussed in Chapter 3. You hire consultants who consider you as their customer. In turn, you should consider the business managers as your customers. Somewhere in the definition of facility terms the letters "c," "t," "o," and "m" were dropped from *customers* to form "users." Thus, corporate businesses are usually referred to as users.

While the idea of not needing daily planning is nice to think about, there is very little chance of eliminating it. The rush project is a result of real business changes in the market, circumstances beyond one's control, surprise reorganizations, and, in some cases, bad luck. When business managers deliberately wait for the last moment, the situation should be escalated to the next level of management for resolution. This is a highly political but practical way to resolve unprofessional behavior. The business manager and the facility manager *do* work for the same corporation. This fact disappears from the business manager's thought process. Business managers must be convinced that facility managers are a resource.

Components of the master space plan process

Reviewed below are components of the master space plan, including information on real property and a business unit's requirements. Financial forecasting and budgeting—essential to support the master plan—are discussed in Chapter 4.

Real property criteria.   The facility manager commences the process by assessing occupancy and known changes in existing buildings. The existing occupancy should be analyzed with groupings of corporate functions in mind, divided among space needs for public contact, support functions, and business needs.

- Requirements of public contact space.
    - Quick and easy access from the street.
    - Convenient access to public transportation.
    - Security solution to allow the public in without compromising the integrity of the building.
    - Primary location on street level.
    - Secondary location from one floor below street level to three floors above street.

- Types of public contact spaces.
    - Retail stores and shops.
    - Restaurants.
    - Personnel departments.
    - General employment and testing offices.
    - Professional or college recruitment offices.
    - Corporate medical departments.
    - Branches of banks and utilities.
    - Public amenities, including atria and through-block arcades, provided at street level

- Requirements of support space.
    - Minimal changes in location, once constructed.
    - Large square footage in relationship to number of staff located within the space

- Daily access to a truck dock or to the street.
- Floors with higher load-bearing capacity.
- Less expensive rent.
- Security.
- Primary location one to three floors below street level.

- Types of support spaces.
  - Branch back-office support staff.
  - Large computer facilities (you'll get disagreement from corporate safety staff on the location since they may claim potential water damage).
  - Vaults for storage of precious metals, money, securities, jewelry.
  - Telecommunications equipment.
  - Building management functions.
  - Building security.
  - Building mechanical equipment.
  - Tenant storage.
  - Cafeterias and other employee amenities. Cafeterias are frequently located above grade owing to emotional consideration rather than good planning. Such locational decisions may lead to problems in elevator use and demands for better use of prime, windowed, higher-floor office space.
  - Support space can be above street level when below-grade space is limited, below-grade space is nonexistent, space above street level has no windows, or space above street level has limited or no views.
  - First priority must go to building support functions and public space support functions when below-street space is limited. The second priority should be tenant storage.

- Requirements of a business unit's space.
  - Clear signage identifying how to gain access to the department.
  - Appropriate image for the employees and the customers.
  - Enough space to allow for the smooth flow of work.
  - Sufficient room for planned changes in staffing (this may be horizontal growth on the same floor, or vertical growth on adjoining floors).
  - Adjacency to other departments that have daily interaction.
  - Business plan as the basis for needs including staff projections.

Business plans must be interpreted into a facility manager's standard means of measurement: square footage. This process of converting written business plans into square footage is captured in the programming phase of a project. Programming is reviewed in Chapter 4.

Space assigned to the businesses is usually shown to senior management in a stacking plan, which is covered next.

1.3 Stacking

Because of the reorganization, the basement will be on the second floor. One-half of the second floor will be on the first floor. But, one-half will remain on the second floor. The first floor will move to the basement.

This is the "official" whimsical language used by all facility managers. Although the floor numbers change from time to time, this language avoids the names of individual departments. Additionally, the timing of moves and amount of corporate expenditures are not mentioned. Yet this phrase, once stated, is understood by all parties involved with the changes.

Hidden meanings in this simple phrase are:

- Senior management has approved a reorganization.

- Moves and sequences are approved by management.

- Plan will realign staff under new corporate management.

- Questions may be directed to the facility manager—now responsible for the changes.

- Funding has been approved to accomplish these moves.

- It is now reestablished that other managers will not want your job!

Stacking defined

After 20-plus years of using this language, I decided to set the facility managers straight by turning to the dictionary. The dictionary is never wrong. It is the official book that defines each and every word with its exact meaning. I'll be using *The World Book Dictionary* as the source for definitions throughout the text.

"Stacking" is defined as "the circling of an airport by aircraft in a controlled pattern while awaiting landing instructions." This definition does not suit our purpose, so let's review the meaning of "stack": "an orderly pile, heap, or group of anything."

A definition for "combined facility" should read: "a group of departments circling a building awaiting the facility manager's instructions for floor assignments that will result in an orderly heap according to the corporate organizational structure." A stacking plan is a method of reporting to management the current or future occupancy of business units within a given building or buildings.

Where we are (WWA).   The current stacking plan shows each and every unit, by floor, with the exact square-foot occupancy. Each unit is shown in scale. This is done to provide a quick visualization of each department's size in relationship to the others (see Figures 1.1 and 1.2).

15	
14	
13	
12	
11	
10	
9	
8	
7	
6	
5	
4	
3	
2	Mechanical
1	
Concourse	
Subcellar	

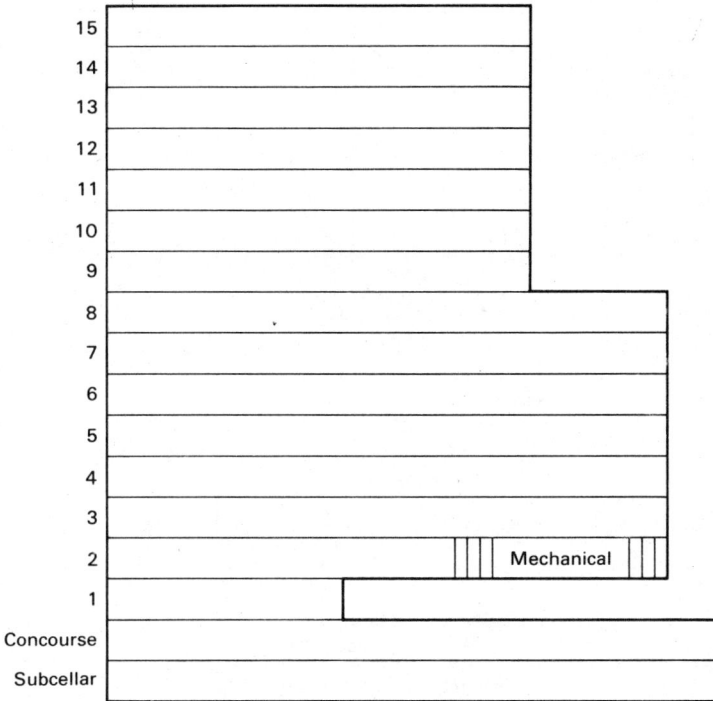

Figure 1.1   Yourco place blank stacking plan.

Where we want to be (WWWTB).   The future plan shows the planned final location of the business units that remain in the building. The scale of the units to each other is maintained. If square footage is shown next to each unit, the facility manager should follow these rules:

- Show exact square footage for the units that did not change.
- Use a rounded square footage for any units that show a change (up or down) in occupancy.
- Use an exact square footage when the unit occupies all the space on a floor, or all remaining space on a floor.

Rounded occupancy numbers highlight to senior management the nature of forecasting as opposed to an exact science. An example: The forecast for a department, based on a written program, is 12,532 square feet. The assigned floor is 20,000 square feet and totally vacant. The facility manager may show the occupancy as 12,532 square feet with 7468 vacant on the floor; rounded to 12,500 and 7500, respectively; or rounded to the nearest thousand, 12.5 M and 7.5 M vacant. In the last case, "M" means thousands. (The use of the initial K is usu-

15	Executive administration	
14	Legal department	
13	Mortgage department	
12	Mortgage department	
11	Commercial letter of credit	
10	Human resources	Vacant
9	Corporate real estate	Facilities
8	Credit division (dept. A, B, C, D)	
7	Credit division	
6	Customer service; credit division	
5	Corporate finance department	
4	Corporate finance dept.	Sales division
3	International	International trading
2	International department	Mechanical
1	Branch	Retail	Personnel
Concourse	Branch support	Vault	Medical	Security/ bldg. off.
Subcellar	Cafeteria	Lounge	Finance data center

Figure 1.2 Yourco place current occupancy, October 1988.

ally reserved to mean thousands of dollars.) A double "M" (MM) would be used for millions.

How we get there (HWGT).   There may be one or more interim stacking plans to show progress moves between the existing plans and future plans. The occupancy status of the building or buildings, at particular intervals during the master plan's restacking sequence, are shown on the plans. These intervals can be based on:

- Year-end dates when several years are required to accomplish the sequence
- Monthly or bimonthly dates when fewer than 24 months are required for the sequence
- Completion of significant moves—when a major move is accomplished or a major occupancy change occurs

Senior management can easily review the occupancy of a building, in any time period, on a single page. The color computer monitor is great, but senior managers usually do not visit your workstation for presentations.

Stacking plans can be as simple as a typed listing of floors with departmental names next to each floor number. However, most stacking plans have the outline of the building drawn with horizontal lines separating each floor from the next. More sophisticated stacking plans have the departments color-coded by organizational groups or divisions.

Color plans allow senior management to quickly assess occupancy by group, business manager, or functions. The use of color always helps sell a plan. Management follows the stacking sequences (WWA, WWWTB, and HWGT) by noting the colors coming together on adjacent floors over time. Facility managers must be able to use color photocopying techniques, when required, to produce multiple sets. If color copying cannot be accomplished, two alternatives are available:

- Hand-colored originals.
- Black-and-white patterns to show the different groups and divisions. Facility managers may use dots, lines, and stripes running vertically or angled. The use of the photocopier now makes possible multiple reproductions.

Stacking plans: Used and abused.   Stacking plans are used to analyze:

- Future moves
- Units which must relocate to accommodate another unit's planned expansion
- General information for space inventory and allocations
- Planned vacancies to allow for future assignments or sublets
- Planned space shortfalls to plan for future rentals for displaced units
- Which unit plotting business managers request for relocating to allow for their own expansion.

Some business managers have the knack of abusing the plan just by dropping a word to senior management on the lack of profitability of the other unit that is in the way of their expansion. A simple rule to follow, adoptable by your corporation, is financial accountability. This eliminates the abuse of stacking plans and may decrease some of the unnecessary changes that occur.

Financial accountability.   Relocation funding is handled differently among corporations. A common practice is for each department or business to be financially accountable for its profit and loss—the bottom line.

Senior management changes. Restacks that result from a reorganization or other senior management change should be funded by senior management. They fund the project directly or indirectly. Direct payment is usually done by establishing a separate project budget. The facility manager's forecast is the basis for the funding amount. The facility manager is responsible for the expenditures. The indirect method of funding is by an amount allotted to the individual department. The department manager and facility manager are jointly responsible for managing costs. Senior management may elect not to transfer funds but may recognize the expenditures as an approved overrun of the original departmental budget.

Business management changes. When a business unit moves at the demand of another business, the unit forcing the move picks up the costs. This means that the expansion must be covered by the expanding unit's planned income. This funding method is expensive for the growing unit, but it is the "price to pay" for poor forecasting. Units being relocated always try negotiating for new items, such as furniture. The funding is to replace in kind the facilities of the unit being relocated. The cost to write off undepreciated assets is charged to the unit forcing the move.

Master plan changes. The funding method for moves required by the master plan is up to senior management. Usually, moves in a future period can be included in the department's budget for that year. Required moves that occur before the budget cycle are handled in the same manner as the senior management changes shown previously.

The fourth dimension of time

Facility managers need complete working knowledge of width, length, and height for solving practical problems. Most important is the ability to think in the fourth dimension of time. You must anticipate how a current space will be used in *all* future periods of the master space plan. This reduces future furniture and construction costs as well as relocation expenses. A space may be used several times for interim departmental "camp outs" that are moved to clear space for another unit's relocation.

Senior management's review of stacking plans may also reveal highly confidential information to the facility manager. Political changes, reorganizations, dissolution or creation of businesses, and mergers of functions are among the many bits of information that may be interpreted from reading stacking plans. Facility managers are required to keep this information confidential. Facility managers are also required to make all assignments of space in an impartial manner. This is particularly difficult when a relocation or a space assignment affects the facility manager's own division.

Stacking plans versus rumored reorganizations. Reorganization rumors hit the facility manager with shocking force. Facility managers may use the rumor as an ally or as an enemy to maintain sanity on the job. You get calls from business managers seeking confirmation or denial of the rumor. This is not an occasion for bartering.

Rumors frustrate facility managers—changes are occurring without any planning input. You seek to be ready by immediately drafting new stacking plans. Of course, the rumored reorganization may never occur. The best advice for the facility manager is not to add fuel to the fire.

Facility managers must wait for the confirmed change. Senior management always has the right to make business changes. The facility manager's opinion on the practical physical changes may not have bearing on the overall corporate changes required.

Real reorganizations seem to occur at the end of a fiscal year, after a bad quarter, or after a senior officer's vacation. At all other times, the reorganization is just a rumor. Rumors may be the ally of the facility manager. You do not make irrational statements. You stand still when others are running around scrambling for confirmation. Rumors are your enemy when senior management totally excludes you from the process. The credibility of your position is somewhat reduced.

Stacking plans versus real reorganizations. The best way to strengthen the facility manager's position is the real reorganization, if handled properly; otherwise, it may be your worst enemy. This is not a contradiction of terms.

When the real reorganization occurs, the facility manager will be part of senior management's advance team. The facility manager gathers all required information as quickly as possible. Facility managers, in fact, become power brokers. Facility managers are planning, negotiating, and stacking the building(s) to accommodate the changes.

Facility managers make occupancy decisions and master space plan changes in a fairly short period of time. The enemies list grows quickly with perceived bad space assignments. Facility managers should try to resolve all conflicts. However, senior management must be the final arbiter. Business managers bring the rationale for objecting to a stacking plan to a meeting. Facility managers bring the stacking plan and the appropriate rationale.

The facility manager, just like a defense attorney, should be prepared to defend the stacking plan. Senior management brings to a meeting the right to make a decision.

In the eyes of senior management, the best case always wins. Facility managers should be confident, but be prepared for rejection. Rejection is not a personal issue. If you feel it is, change careers now.

Stacking plan rejections.   Some of the reasons senior management rejects stacking plans are as follows:

- Facility manager did not make the correct assumptions, and the stacking plans are not accurate. In other words, you made a mistake; admit it, and correct it.

- Facility manager was given incorrect information, and the stacking plan reflects it. In other words, a business manager's views of the reorganization were incorrect. It is also possible that the facility manager was told a *lie*. Always be prepared to explain the source of your information to senior management. This is not meant to "get" the offending business manager but rather to get the right information. Don't push the inaccuracy beyond a simple explanation.

- Facility manager was correct in all assumptions, but there was more than one way to stack a building. Senior management chose the other solution. No problem for the prepared facility manager. Simply pull out the second set of plans you prepared with the alternate solution. Be prepared to explain your reasons for one plan over the other. You will find that management listens.

- Senior management doesn't give you a reason for rejecting a plan. You react according to your experience level and time spent in the corporation.

Further reasons stacking plans are rejected are:

Freshman facility managers.   Probably explains the stacking plan just as in the opening lines of this section. Senior management likes to hear names of affected departments and business managers.

Sophomore facility managers.   Will gently inquire for reasons, suggest how the plan, as proposed, would work, and then make the changes requested.

Junior facility managers.   Ask senior management for specific reasons or points of disagreement used in rejecting the plan. Offer positive reasons, if any, for the original plan. When all reasons are exhausted, then make the changes.

Senior facility managers.   Did not get to this point by making errors, so the plan is at least 90 percent accurate, with only minor space changes required. Have senior management suggest which method of restacking they would prefer, and be prepared to outline why the plan was not shown in that manner. Ask for another opportunity to review the total impact of requested changes before submitting a final plan.

The facility manager's ability to restack a building uses current occupancy as the basis for planning.

Facility managers should know the following specific pertinent information about current occupancy:

- Where each and every unit is located.

- How much space that unit occupies in both usable and rentable square feet.

- Attributes of the space itself, including when it was built, how it is furnished, type of space, condition of area.

- Name of a senior contact in the area.

- Unit's organizational structure.

- Unit's priority to remain in the building; 1 priority—must remain in building; 2 priority—must remain within one or two blocks of building or on the same campus; 3 priority—must remain in the same city; and 4 priority—may move anywhere

Facility managers have this information stored both in their computer and in their minds; it is gathered through a space inventory—reviewed in the next section.

1.4 Space Inventory

I always worked for large corporations. During my teenage years, when menial jobs were common, I sought out the premiere *corporate position. I was a produce clerk for a major food chain and a stock clerk for a major department store chain.*

Those early jobs had a lot in common with the role of facility manager. In the comparison below, I'll skip the obvious reference to low pay, working behind the scenes, and having to clean up after someone else's mess.

Produce clerk	Stock clerk	Facility manager
Space Planning		
Planned for best use of limited shelf space available to display fruits and vegetables.	Planned and stocked the shelves both on the selling floor and behind the scenes.	Planned for the greatest and best use of office space.

Produce clerk	Stock clerk	Facility manager
	Space Planning	
Always made sure all items were visible and in reach of the customer.	Always allowed sufficient space for planned deliveries.	Tried to maintain enough vacant space to meet unknown changes.
Each item had sufficient space commensurate with sales.	Tried not to leave vacant shelf space because it produced no revenue.	
	Stacking	
Always stacked the fruits and vegetables to ensure that they did not fall or become unstable when a few were removed.	In the days before plastic packaging, I had to stack glass bottles. This required careful planning to ensure soundness of the stack so that bottles would not topple when a few were removed (sold).	Placed public contact areas on or near street level.
Always gave the freshest fruit the best position in the middle of the pile (no one buys the top pieces anyway).		Placed support spaces below grade.
		Placed businesses on upper floors in the building.
	Always stacked similar products near each other.	Stacked units according to adjacency and business relationships.
		Ensured that the plan stood even if a few units were removed.
	Inventory	
Counting oranges, watermelons, grapefruit, and tomatoes was ridiculous. It was easier to count the box or crate prior to opening.	The store always had a preinventory sale that brought in customers—unfortunately, never enough to move all the remaining uncounted tubes of toothpaste. Bar coding would have been a great time saver.	Always had to keep inventory of each unit and the square footage it occupied. Rental costs ranged up to $55 per rentable square foot in New York City and more in London and Tokyo.
Once it was opened, you hoped for all items to sell or to rot—then no need to inventory.	The customer always expected the clerk to know where each and every item was located.	Senior management expected you to know where each unit was located.
The customer (user?) always expected you to know where each and every item was located.		Space had to be managed and controlled.

It is not yet possible to bar-code space. It is possible to track how much a department occupies. Which computer system is the best for space inventory? The answer cannot be given until the facility manager understands what is to be computerized and how the information is gathered.

The computer is a tool to help organize, store, and report information already gathered. Facility managers must first develop a space inventory tracking system that is easy to utilize, easily understood by business managers, and easy to convert into a computer system.

What comes first—the computer or the methodology? Facility managers who have no methods can use any existing system. This saves time. Normally the system does not directly relate to a corporation's way of doing business. Most computer systems will require software changes to fit into the personality of the corporation. Therefore, I suggest you develop a method first, then find the computer system that best fits. If none can be found, then have the software changed to match your corporate needs. The methodology shown below as one solution can be used by corporations of all sizes.

Getting started

Assume that the business manager does not understand square footage as a measurement tool or how to read a floor plan. It is okay to put the definitions in a planning standards manual or other official corporate document. However, for purposes of collecting inventory data, it does become a nuisance to try to explain the variance.

Some facility managers may have trouble explaining to the business manager the fine differences among the following terms:

Gross square feet.   Total space on a floor as measured from window to window and including all core space in between.

Rentable square feet.   Tenant's pro rata portion of the entire floor, excluding certain core elements that penetrate through the floor to areas above or below.

Usable square feet.   Area on a floor that is occupied by tenant; usually includes space not used by people to sit in, such as corridors and toilet rooms.

Net usable square feet.   Actual occupied space that can be used to house people and related office furniture and equipment.

Make the data gathering as simple and foolproof as possible. I suggest the miniplan approach.

The miniplan approach

- Create a reduced copy of the floor plan. This miniplan shows the outline of the floor, the window mullions, and the essential core elements. These key elements include elevators, lobbies, bathrooms, and any core storage rooms available on the floor (see Figure 1-3).

- Miniplan should be no larger than 8½ by 11 inches in size.

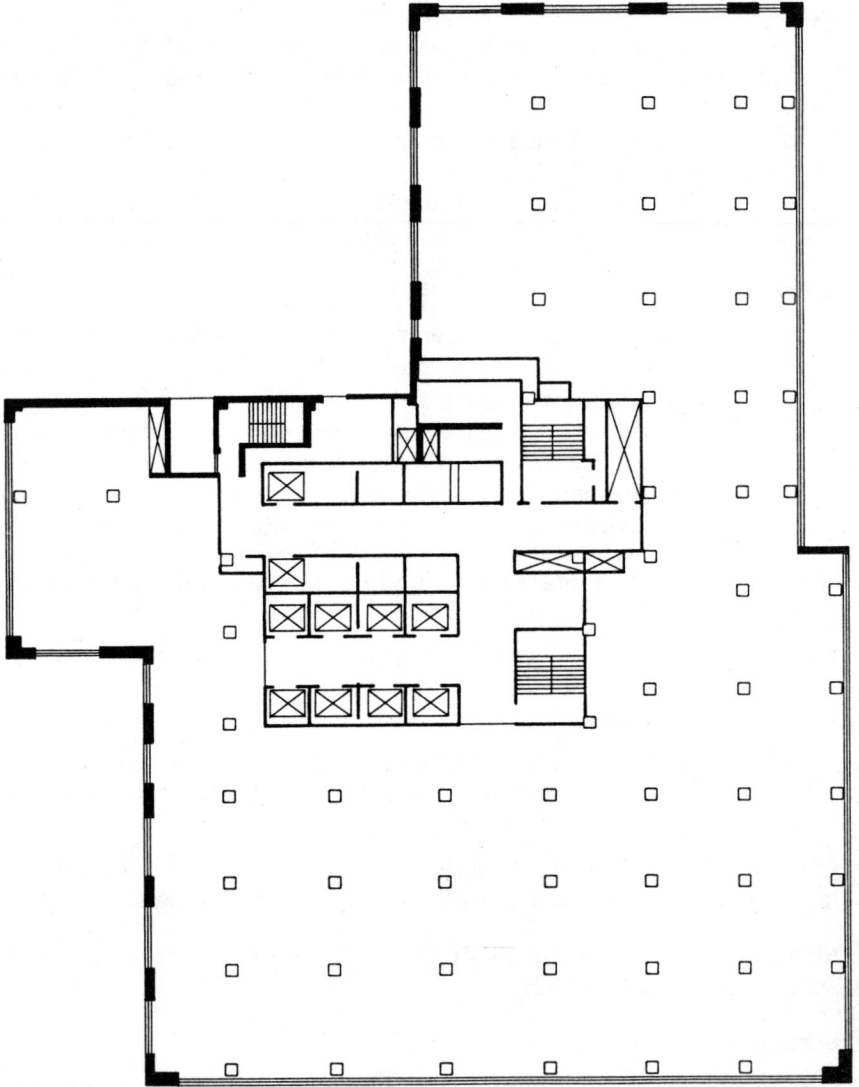

Figure 1.3 Yourco place, eighth floor; blank miniplan.

- Clearly label plan with the building name, the floor, and the amount of square footage that is chargeable for the entire floor (normally this is rentable square feet).

- Do not show any furniture layouts, constructed walls, or lighting patterns. Basically, the plan is blank within the floor outline.

- Divide the plan into a grid pattern. This pattern can be any convenient footage. In buildings that have a 5-foot module, use a 5 by 5 grid. In buildings that have no grid, use a grid that divides the floor equally. It is not essential that the grid align with the window mullions, although it does make the facility manager's task simpler if it does.

- Cover all areas on the floor that can be occupied with the grid. If the facility manager excludes the main corridors from the grid, then the square foot allotment per grid module will increase slightly.

- Count the number of grid modules on the floor.

- Divide the number of grid modules into total square feet to be charged out. This results in a measurement of square feet per module. For example: if the floor has 23,500 rentable square feet, and there are 741 modules on the floor, then there are 31.7 square feet per grid module (see Figure 1.4).

- Forward plan to each user coordinator on the floor.

- Have user coordinators outline the space occupied by their respective groups to the nearest grid line (see Figure 1.5).

- Have user coordinator enter departmental name and applicable charge code. The user coordinator also will multiple the number of grids times the nominal square foot per grid amount to determine the total square foot assignment for the group.

- Have user coordinator forward the signed and dated plan back to you.

- Inspect the plan for accuracy and completeness. Any questionable names or charge codes can be resolved on the telephone.

- Watch out for a space overlap—two adjoining departments claiming the same grid modules. Meet with both user coordinators to determine who is physically occupying the area. This is very important to resolve since possession is everything.

- Watch out for a space underlap—neither adjoining department claiming an area between them. Usually occurs when there is a corridor used by both groups but neither one wants to pay for the space. A common corridor can be split via a zigzag pattern. If the disputes is still unresolved, then the common space could be "de-gridded" and become chargeable to both occupants through a slight increase in

5- X 5-ft grid; 25 usable sq ft
5- X 5-ft grid; 31.7 rentable sq ft

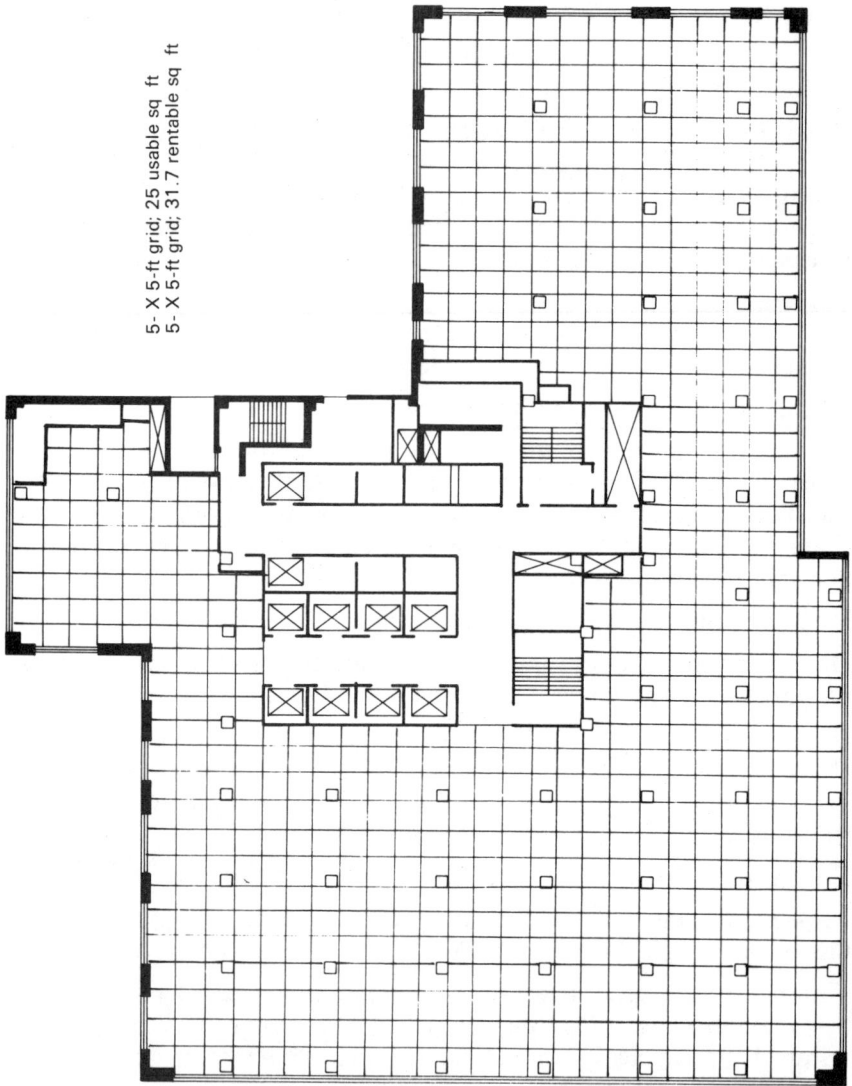

Figure 1.4 Yourco place, eighth floor; miniplan with grid.

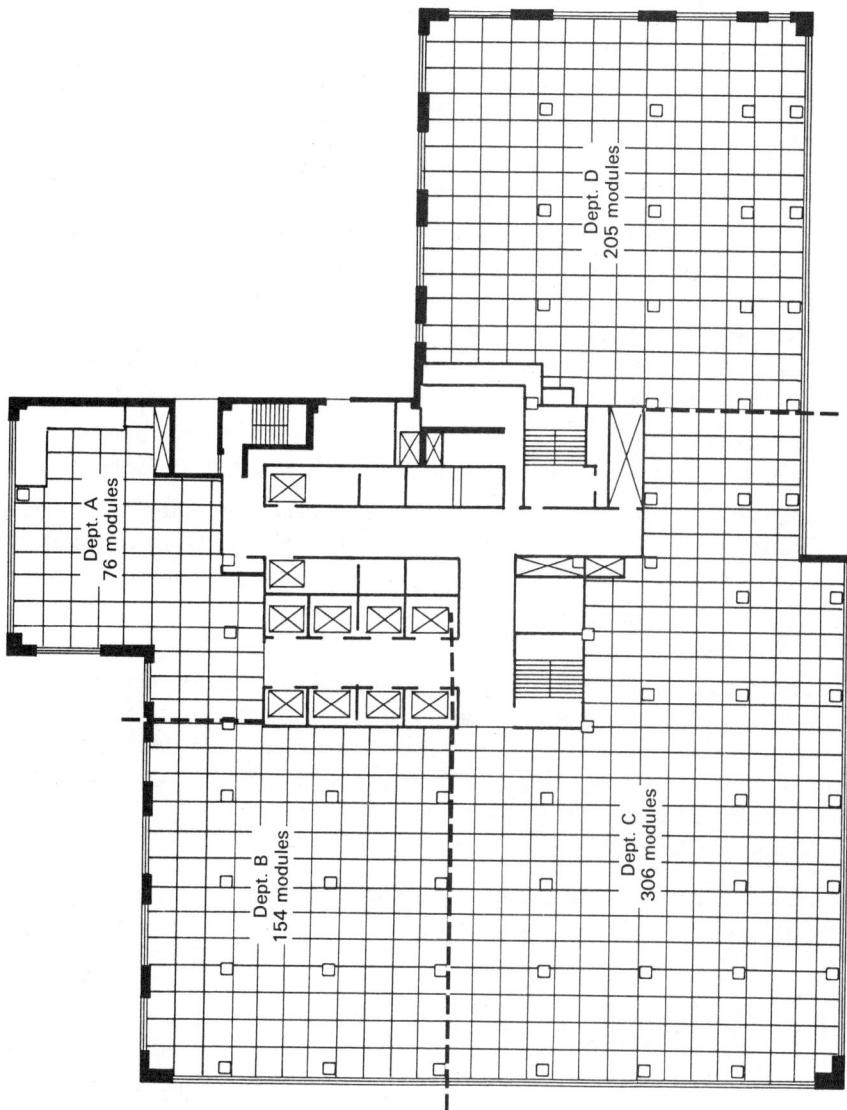

Figure 1.5 Yourco place, eighth floor; miniplan with allocations.

Dept. A
76 modules

Dept. B
154 modules

Dept. C
306 modules

Dept. D
205 modules

23

the square foot assignment per grid. (The number of grids is reduced, creating a higher allocation per module.)

- Final approved miniplans are ready for you to utilize for inventory and reporting. Computer systems which have some degree of computer-aided design can easily store the data that has been captured.

- Create a file on a word processor or prepare a report manually if no computer system exists.

- Space inventory report should reflect the building, the floor, and the amount of square footage occupied by each group on the floor.

- Forward a new blank miniplan for the user coordinator to update after a major relocation or move.

- Report frequency is up to the facility manager and the corporation. Minimum reporting time should be once a year. For corporations with quarterly reporting, the space inventory should be done four times per year. Ambitious facility managers may want 12 reports a year. This is generally too much information and normally is not required by the corporation.

- Convert the finished report into an updated current stacking plan. It always pays to be prepared for that next reorganization.

- Analyze reorganizations as soon as they occur. Frequently, reorganizations do not require physical movement but rather a reclassification of divisional affinity.

What to charge

You now have a method to gather and capture accurate occupancy information. You must tally what is to be charged out to the various user groups. Basic charges to be allocated are common costs in the operation of the building. Charges incurred as a result of the user should be directly charged to the user.

Direct charges are:

- Renovation costs and associated depreciation

- Write-offs of undepreciated assets

- New furniture purchases

- Electrical charges, requiring a separate meter for each floor or major tenant

- Costs associated with the running of the individual business, including personnel, advertising, and training

- Special rental charges, including roof space, basement space, and any other space that may not be measurable

Common building charges should be shared among all tenants. Common charges include:

- Rental expenses.
- Utilities that are not charged directly to the user, such as heating, water, sewer, and electric charges.
- General maintenance and repairs for the building, its grounds, the base building mechanical systems.
- Custodial expenses for rubbish removal and cleaning.
- Salaries and related personnel expenses for the base building office staff.
- Cafeteria and dining room charges are normally charged out on a head-count basis. However, these costs can be charged out on a square foot basis if the corporation prefers this method.

Once all known costs have been forecast, a final allocation number is calculated. Total costs to maintain and run the facility are divided by the total square footage in the building(s). The resultant number is the cost per square footage allocation charge. The allocation charge is multiplied by the amount of square feet each unit occupies to arrive at an allocation charge per group. The allocation process should be done prior to the corporation's annual budget cycle. This allows each group to include occupancy charges in their forecast for the following year.

1.5 The Words of Others—Space and the Use of Computers

Marshall A. Graham, CMC *President, Graham Consulting, Inc.*

All too often in the corporate world, facilities managers have not felt that their role was one of strategic planner, but rather that it was to determine space requirements and to lay out space on the basis of information, lack of information, or misinformation about staffing and functions for the department of the company.

It is refreshing to see the approach suggested in this chapter, that the facilities manager should become part of the middle- and long-range planning functions (micro- and macroplanning).

In this section, I would like to add several remarks about each of the segments of the chapter discussed by the author.

Planning

Building stacking

Space inventory

First, I would like to comment on the role, or lack of role, of the computer in the planning, building stacking, and space inventory process. Planning is not new. Strategic planning and tracking of facilities use were carried out by the forerunners of our present-day facilities manager in some form long before computers were made part of our working environment. I remember the hours and days spent in front of an electric calculator, tabulating statistics and space uses.

Today, the computer is becoming indispensable to most fields of business and for many aspects of personal life. Use of the computer is as diverse as there are functions in business operations. As part of this diversity, computer applications have been developed to assist the facilities manager in planning for and in maintaining facilities. Even though not identified specifically, all of the elements described in this chapter for the planning functions lend themselves to computer use—whether statistical, database, or graphic.

Planning

Years ago, the method for planning office space for a company or a new office building included the development of rough estimates of size. For new construction, too often, the decision for establishing the size of a building—the floor area and number of floors—was based on the architect's maximizing the building size for the site that had already been preselected. In the case of planning for office space in multitenant buildings already designed, a space may first be leased, and then staff and departments forced into the space.

Gradually, during the past 20 years, planning has developed into a strategic science as business practices and administration have improved. As projects increase in size and complexity, more extensive documentation is required to justify the need, size, and cost of the project. To develop and update that type of data by hand has become a formidable task, resulting in the more extensive use of computers.

In addition to such factors as space standards and types of space to be planned for (discussed later in this book), following are several major factors to be considered in the planning phase of a facilities project:

- Organization structure
- Staff forecasting
- Department adjacencies

Organization. For years, architects and planners have stated that "a major factor to consider in facilities planning is that *form follows function.*" Function in a company or institution is best personified in both the macro and the micro sense by its organization structure. To develop an understanding of any organization and to maintain control of all operations and units of that organization during the planning stages, a complete organization chart should be obtained by the facility manager or, if it is not available, should be prepared.

At the least, a listing of all departments and departmental subdivisions or units should be prepared and kept up to date. This information not only is useful for the planning stages but becomes the basis for most staffing, facilities, and furniture information about the company that the facilities manager makes use of.

Some of the newer computer programs for use in facilities management have integrated this charting ability within the computer's statistical database for staff, space, and furniture control.

Staff forecasting.   We should try hard not to forget that organizations are made up of units or functions that are staffed by *people*. Facilities are the package in which these human resources reside for their working life. One of the most difficult tasks for any company is to project its staffing requirements. Even in the case of daily planning—as difficult as this task is, and the foibles of which have been described earlier— department managers not only report an emergency space problem but also try to have added space prepared for an often off-the-cuff forecast of increases or decreases in staff.

At best, any forecasting of staff as the basis for facilities planning will be an educated guess. However, in the absence of a perfect crystal ball, this educated guess is better than no analysis at all. For this purpose, there are several techniques that have been helpful.

- Trending historical growth patterns and extrapolating these data into the future using straight line, central tendency, or weighted average forecasting techniques.

- Relating staff to production, sales, or marketing records or forecasts and extrapolating trends to the future.

- Relating executive and management staffs to operating staffs on the basis of work load and supervisory control standards.

One technique that I have found to be successful adds to these methods a system of "control totals" applied to all segments of the company. This method, which can be used for either micro- or macroplanning, works as follows:

- If an organization has several hierarchical levels, first determine the *total* projected numbers of staff for the *total* organization using one of the techniques mentioned above.

- Then, using this number as a control (control total), determine the projections for each of the second hierarchical levels of the organization's divisions.

- Next, using the control total for each of these divisions, determine the total staff projections for each group of departments within each division for the next hierarchical level, and continue this approach to the lowest level of units within the organization.

- At that point, supervisors of those units are given the control total of staff that they will be allowed by management and are asked to distribute those staff positions among the job categories needed to operate their organizational units. It will be the supervisors' responsibility to distribute their staff positions consistent with the functions they must carry out, and with the budget they have available for their departmental operations.

To be successful, every micro- and macroplan forecasting method requires at least the following elements:

- Methods for gathering information
- Statistical method that is used on a continuing basis, so that comparison data can be provided for extended periods
- Method for gaming the data (answering a series of "what if" questions)
- Imagination
- And, above all—*luck*

Obviously, the further into the future one projects, the less secure can be the level of confidence in the results. However, the results will turn out to be, at best, reasonably accurate and, at worst, better than no estimate at all.

Finally, when establishing any micro- or macroplan, it is interesting to establish ranges of forecasts. It sounds as if such an approach is a method for facilities managers to hedge their bets. However, if ranges of forecasts are presented with adequate and well-thought-out scenarios upon which they are based, they can be extremely useful in the final decision-making process by top management of the organization.

Through the procedure of "computer gaming," it has become possible to evaluate unlimited numbers of variations in space requirements that may affect the building process. As a result of the modeling of alternate space size standards for staff levels, equipment, and functions, the computer can produce comparative data in summary form in minutes. From these data, computer graphics comparison charts and graphs can be produced, in black-and-white, in color, or as presentation slides. The use of some of the better-developed decision support systems (DSS) software can be helpful (see Figure 1.6).

Space requirements report. The results of the steps listed above can be generated as a computer printout, either on the computer's CRT screen or on paper. These printouts are produced from the database of the space standards applied to the database of the information on staff, equipment, functions, standards, and circulation factors. Because they are computer-based, these reports can be generated in varying levels of detail for the three major levels of management—supervisor, middle management, and top management.

- For the *facilities manager,* these reports must be in complete detail, showing facilities implications for every person, function, and item of equipment for which space must be provided.

- For *supervisory level* staff and for the facilities management departments, these reports should also be in detail for each department manager to use in verifying each detail of staff, equipment, and special function for space to be planned and allocated for the department.

- For *middle management,* reports would be produced in summary form by division, or groups of departments, for which they are responsible. In addition, the many computer programs can provide data in many different formats to provide specialized information for the middle manager and for the facilities manager. These special reports can include tabulations of the number of each office space standard and special piece of equipment that will require floor space. This information will allow the planner to consider alternate sizes or alternate operating practices that can affect the space requirements for the future. For example, calculations of the locations and amounts of files, together with the amount of space that they take up, can provide management with information that, as a result of a cost-benefits analysis, may result in the need for development of a records management system that can eliminate the number of files and records storage rooms (and therefore reduce space needs) that exist or will be planned for the future.

- For *top management,* broader-scale summary reports that show concepts and overall patterns of growth are desirable. The computer programs should have the capability to produce these types of summary reports, together with graphic representations of the totals, as well as the detail types of reports described above.

Department adjacencies. Department adjacencies can be determined in several ways. One method used by the writer a number of years ago consisted of a computerized traffic survey. All the employees of a large

Figure 1.6 Yourco comparison of alternate space standards; Environetics.

DEPARTMENT	STAFF 1987	STAFF 1992	ALTERNATE A 1987	ALTERNATE A 1992	ALTERNATE B 1987	ALTERNATE B 1992	ALTERNATE C 1987	ALTERNATE C 1992
HQ1A EXECUTIVE - HEADQUARTERS	8	11	4,534	5,284	4,965	5,851	5,006	5,877
SUBTOTAL	8	11	4,534	5,284	4,965	5,851	5,006	5,877
HQ2 LAW - OFFICE OF SENIOR VICE PRESIDENT	15	21	1,639	2,055	2,102	2,657	2,650	3,346
HQ2A LAW - LITIGATION	19	26	1,867	2,353	2,344	2,994	2,872	3,662
HQ2B LAW - GENERAL LAWS	22	30	2,207	2,915	2,811	3,732	3,485	4,611
HQ2C LAW - CONTRACTS	15	21	1,543	2,049	1,965	2,615	2,417	3,207
HQ2D LAW - ADMINISTRATIVE LAWS	21	30	2,201	3,061	2,805	3,915	3,434	4,788
SUBTOTAL	92	128	9,437	12,433	12,027	15,913	14,858	19,614
HQ3 PUBLIC AFFAIRS - OFFICE OF VP	4	7	1,213	1,698	1,565	2,173	1,550	2,284
HQ3A1 PUBLIC AFFAIRS - MEDIA RELATIONS	26	32	3,744	4,293	4,415	5,138	4,885	5,666
HQ3B PUBLIC AFFAIRS - NEW PROJ & EVENTS	13	17	1,678	2,032	2,217	2,676	2,371	2,934
HQ3C PUBLIC AFFAIRS - CORPORATE HISTORY	7	11	1,081	1,495	1,417	5,469	1,243	5,304
HQ3D PUBLIC AFFAIRS - CREATIVE SERVICES	18	23	2,845	3,699	3,772	4,921	3,117	3,985
HQ3F PUBLIC AFFAIRS - INTERGOVT REL & POLI	26	35	3,024	4,051	3,922	5,323	4,598	5,984
SUBTOTAL	94	125	13,585	20,731	17,308	25,700	17,764	26,157
GROUP SUBTOTAL	194	264	27,556	36,448	34,300	47,464	37,628	51,648
HQ4 FINANCE - OFFICE OF SENIOR VICE PRES	4	7	774	1,189	969	1,487	1,196	
HQ4A FINANCE - DATA PROCESSING	13	24	3,662	4,719	4,291	5,552		14,430
HQ4B FINANCE - CONTROLLER/ACCOUNTING	46	64	5,453	6,956	7,293	9,35_	5,998	5,998
HQ4C FINANCE - INSURANCE	7	9	347	347				
HQ4D FINANCE - DISBURSEMENT AUTHORIZATION	11	15	1,183	1,708				
HQ4E FINANCE - ACCOUNTS PAYABLE	8	12	508					
HQ4F FINANCE - CORPORATE FINANCE	17	23	...6		6_,215		65,099	73,160
SUBTOTAL			3,131	3,971	1,401	1,401	1,535	1,535
HQ5A3 SYSTEM OPERATIONS	15	529	26,706	30,250	4,290	5,429	4,408	5,851
... SERVICES	72	94	1,329	1,632	34,251	38,897	39,045	44,536
...CONTRACT ADMIN - OFF OF	7	7	12,575	14,244	1,836	2,268	2,274	2,824
PROCUREMENT & CONTRACT ADMIN - CONTRA	48	59	800	800	16,456	18,679	15,649	18,204
... PROCUREMENT & CONTRACT ADM	4	7	2,575	2,991	1,000	1,000	1,214	1,214
BR9D PROCURE & CONTR ADMIN	5	8	354	810	3,627	4,234	4,674	5,465
BR9E CORPORATE SUPPORT SERVICES	32	40	2,134	2,651	461	1,030	563	1,246
SUBTOTAL	503	610	54,139	62,616	70,541	81,771	76,089	89,445
GROUP SUBTOTAL	1428	1773	186,835	214,398	240,436	277,433	253,588	296,413
GRAND TOTAL	1622	2037	214,391	252,846	274,736	324,897	291,216	348,061

30

organization were asked to take a prepunched IBM card every time they visited another department, and to drop the card at the department visited. (The same method was used for every document that was sent to other departments.) When tallied, the results showed the number or extent of traffic between departments and, by logic, the adjacency relationships that should prescribe the location in the building for each department.

Not so! Discussions with top level management defined other adjacency relationships that were even stronger than the "card-carrying" technique. Therefore, in most studies today, adjacency requirements are determined by interview with knowledgeable managers, adjacency matrixes are prepared, and these become the basis for the stacking and floor layout plans only after review with top management of the organization.

Building stacking

In this chapter, it was good to see discussion of cost responsibility and the participation of the facilities manager in the planning function, two major elements in planning.

First, the application of cost responsibility for the development of stacking plans for an organization is a must. In most reporting systems, the stack showing reorganization of a facility as result of changes in a company's human and functional requirements is presented as a design function. It is the responsibility of the facilities manager to carefully relate that design recommendation to the cost of attaining it. Then, in line with the practice of the company, the charges for the moves would be allocated to the segment of business where it belonged. But the decision for the move would be based on complete facts—functional, physical and financial.

Second, there is a need for the facility manager to be an integral part of the planning loop. If not, the loop could look like a hula hoop, continually rotating, and eventually dropping to the ground with little or no tangible results. As a part of the planning process, and when reorganization on a proactive basis is being considered, the facilities churn can be kept to a minimum. And when it is necessary, at least it will be based on planned logic rather than on frustrating reactions.

At the end of the section on stacking, Mr. Binder includes an extensive list of information that the facility manager should maintain about each department in the building (or buildings). Not to belabor the point of computerization, there are several simple and low-cost computer programs that will allow the facility manager to enter and keep track of the amount of space, the type of space, and many attributes of that space and its people and equipment for all of the buildings under his or her jurisdiction.

Facility managers should become knowledgeable about these programs, and then can decide if the size or complexity of their facility resources would warrant the need of such assistance. As a rule of thumb, if the facilities exceed 250,000 square feet, and if there are more than 35 departments for which space information is being maintained, it would be useful to have computerized help in this process. Of course, the size of the facility and the amount of information that one may want to maintain will determine the level of computer that will be required—mainframe, mini, or micro.

Space inventory

The section on space inventory is well thought out and should be included as a major function for the facilities manager. As described by the author, space is never static. The churn (periodic changeover of space as a result of changes in an organization) can range from 10 to 100 percent of the facilities. A usual figure, however, is about 20 to 35 percent per year for the average organization.

Of increasing interest to the facilities manager is the extension of the space inventory to become the basis for an asset management system. Asset management, controlled by the purchasing or financial departments in most organizations in the past, is gradually becoming part of the responsibility of the facilities manager. Therefore, using the definitions included by the author, the facilities manager may even have to become the produce clerk or the stock clerk, and know where every item of produce is located within the space envelope.

Summary

The computer is a tool of incredible strength, speed, and versatility. The facilities manager, space planner, architect, and designer have an opportunity today to add this technology to their bag of tools. Most companies already have one or more microcomputers in use. Programs that can carry out the steps described above are not expensive. With care, proper planning, and staff training, the computer can become an invaluable assistant in the facilities practice for the small, as well as the large, practitioner, and its use should be seriously considered.

2

Standards:
Setting and Selling

2.1 Introduction

How important is it to have corporate standards? Does management even know what they are?

On March 29, 1983, President Reagan signed the Government Workspace Management Reform Executive Order, which required increased management of furnishings and workspaces throughout the federal government. In the case of the U.S. government, the goal was 135 square feet per workstation. No one expects the oval office to be turned into four or five workstations. Nor does one expect the President to pace off the office of a senior accountant in the General Accounting Office. The real objective of the facility managers who were behind that executive order was to secure the seniormost person's approval to reflect to the staff that a commitment has been made.

The task of maintaining that standard is upon the facility managers. The real management goal is cost savings in rental expense and maximum space utilization. Why then does it take the President, or a corporate chairman or equal senior officer to get someone to listen? Perhaps it is a personal issue. While individuals are not personally affected by a corporate goal of 15 percent return on investment, just ask them to reduce their own private workstation by 15 percent. These officers know only one person to vent their anger, disagreement, and frustration upon: the facility manager.

Corporations use standards as a management tool, but the end users look toward the standard as a design tool in solving their special needs. The facility manager serves as the important link between corporate management's goals as to standards and the rest of the corporation's desire to be individualistic. The following sections explore both sides of the issue.

2.2 Standards as a Management Tool

The end of World War II marked a dramatic shift to an office and technological service-oriented environment. The U.S. Department of Labor, Bureau of Statistics, reported that the number of office workers in the work force rose from 20 percent in 1940 to nearly 38 percent in 1987.

With the advent of all these office workers, the task of planning, designing, constructing, and furnishing the space has grown too complex for the "old" office manager, who was an individual not specifically trained for the tasks, but who used available "spare time" to make changes. Prior to the technology boom, the moves were far less complicated and were relatively easy to manage.

In the late 1970s, corporate senior management began stressing improvements in the environment for the worker. In addition to complying with federal and state legislation and local city codes, management saw that productivity gains resulted from increased expenditures for ergonomical and environmental solutions.

Dramatic increases in rental expenses provided a financial reason for management's concerns. In some markets, such as New York City, the methodology for measuring space changed so that a square foot became up to 25 percent larger than in the past! This was achieved when the Real Estate Board of New York decided to allow building owners to calculate space differently.

In many cases, 1980 marked management's recognizing that the office manager's skills fell short. Only a specialist could cope with these technical and financial happenings. Initially, management called in the architectural firms to fill the void. But the architects chose to ignore requests and avoided interior design-related jobs. Interior design firms, too preoccupied with decorative solutions, also avoided new and unusual corporate needs.

The facility management profession was born—or born again, if you prefer—out of corporate necessity and desperation to control the process. Management needed an insider who could understand the needs of the company yet could "talk" architecture, engineering, construction, and furniture. At first, management could not decide how to answer the question: "Where do we house the insider's group organizationally?"

- Premises department? Facility management was definitely born out of it.

- Corporate or strategic planning? The need to deal with business decisions makes it belong here.

- Human resources? The need to know personnel projections makes this the logical organizational solution.

- Operations department? The day-to-day changes in telecommunications and maintenance place facility management here.

- Corporate real estate? Many responsibilities indicate this as the proper selection.
  - New leases to be negotiated.
  - Extension of existing leases to be handled.
  - Work letters to be analyzed.
  - Site locations that need to be inspected.
  - Other related real estate matters.

Anywhere appears to be the best spot as long as the facility manager reports directly either to one of the seniormost officers or to board members. That direct report should ensure a fairly impartial person to serve as final arbiter for space issues.

Selling management

Standards for space and furniture are so politically sensitive that the facility manager must literally calculate the path to approval. The larger the corporation, the more difficult it may be to achieve a uniform standards program. The best case is to secure the approval of the chief executive officer or the president at the outset. This avoids your having to read the rest of this section!

Unfortunately, this is usually not possible and requires additional political savoir faire. After all, why should the president, who didn't get to the top position without political savvy, sign? If the standards reflect reductions in space per person and reduced quality standards, advance approval will be difficult to achieve.

The quality reductions could include less wood, increased painted trims on systems in lieu of chrome, downgraded furniture selections, or fewer items of furniture per office. Furniture savings can be made by substituting fabric instead of leather or two chairs instead of a three-seater couch.

"Ground support" from the various end users who will live with the standards in the future is imperative during the developmental stages of standards setting. If possible, select a senior level person from each major department or division to participate in the standards review process. They will review the facility manager's suggestions rather than get involved in the actual furniture selections. You will find it

TABLE 2.1   Projected Savings in Space Rental for Yourco, Inc.

	Rentable square feet (000s)
1. Current occupancy	3500.0
2. Average 25 percent churn per annum	875.0
3. Assume 50 percent of churn space to get new guidelines balance of space to match existing	437.5
4. Planned new space acquisitions by Yourco this year	80.0
5. Total space subject to reductions	517.5
6. Annual 10 percent space save through use of new standards	51.8
7. Cost of space	
Average base rent: $30.00	
Cleaning/maintenance: $ 6.50	
Total cost of space:	$ 36.50
8. First year's projected rental save (51.8 RSF × $36.50)	$1890.70

virtually impossible to get 15 or 20 individuals to agree on the same thing, but at least they will feel that they participated in the process.

The deviation range of space standards, discussed elsewhere in this chapter, provides a perfect example of resolving personal differences in this review committee. This range allows for a spread of 20 percent from the facility manager's selected square footage allocation without dictating an exact space assignment.

When publishing the standards, remember one imperative: List the groups and the officers who participated in their review and establishment. That select group becomes the facility manager's support for adherence to the standards.

Build a mock-up of the standard. Senior managers often have difficulty visualizing standards, and facility managers must be certain

TABLE 2.2   Projected Savings in Space Rental for Yourco, Inc. 5-Year Space Analysis*

	Rentable square feet (000s)	×	Base rent	+	Cleaning and maintenance	=	Annual rental save ($)
First year:	[51.8]	×	[$30.00	+	$6.50]	=	1890.70
Second year:	[51.8]	×	[$30.00	+	$6.83]	=	1907.79
Third year:	[51.8]	×	[$30.00	+	$7.17]	=	1925.41
Fourth year:	[51.8]	×	[$30.00	+	$7.52]	=	1943.54
Fifth year:	[51.8]	×	[$30.00	+	$7.90]	=	1963.22
5-year projected save in Yourco rental expense						=	9630.66

*Assumptions: No additional space for 5 years, rent remains flat, 5 percent escalation on cleaning and maintenance, and cost of funds is excluded.

that the proposed standard works. Once you settle on a furniture system and square foot allocation, the best advocate of the standard is a sample the prospective end users can sit in, see, and touch.

First invite the review committee *individually* to review, comment, and respond to a questionnaire outlining agreement or concerns. Review the comments, and make whatever changes are appropriate without compromising the standards. Then invite each reviewer back for a final look. Present an economic analysis that outlines the potential saves associated with the new standards. Show potential saves in both rental expenses and furniture expenditures through implementation of the standards.

Table 2.1 reflects a sample analysis for your corporation (Yourco, Inc.). If the facility manager then carries this first year's save out for 5 or 10 years, the save potential really adds up quickly (see Table 2.2).

To assess the saves for furniture and furnishings, an analysis should be compiled for each changed office standard. Table 2.3 reflects such analysis for a middle management workspace that is being reduced in space and in furniture standards.

Pros and Cons of Implementing New Standards

Pros	Cons	Recommendations
Reduction in capital outlay for furniture expenditures	Increased density due to decreased office size may raise ambient noise level and possibly lower productivity	Senior management review and approve new standards because of overriding financial saves (see Table 2.4)
Reduction in space required, which in turn will lower rental expense	Possible decline in staff morale due to perceived inequality from a new area built to new standards versus existing older units at the old standards	Divisional management which has been part of the review process must be responsible for supporting the standards
Slight save in design consultant fees typically based on square footage		

Summary

You can now forward a summary memorandum to senior management outlining the potential saves from rental expense and furniture expenditures and noting that senior officials from different divisions participated in the review and approved the standards. Senior management will have no problem with potential saves and will support anything that these senior officials have agreed to support.

The standards should allow for exceptions. It is recommended that the

TABLE 2.3 Projected Savings in Furniture For Yourco, Inc. Comparison of Current Standards to New Standards Middle Management Level

(Rounded to Nearest Whole Dollar)

Items	Current standards			New standards			Qualitative remarks
	Quantity	Amount ($)	Totals ($)	Quantity	Amount ($)	Totals ($)	
Furniture							
Desk/table	1	600	600	1	550	550	Attractiveness
Desk chair	1	300	300	1	250	250	Features
Visitor chair	3	250	750	2	225	450	Qty/fabric cost
Storage units	2	1200	2400	2	1050	2100	Open bookcase
Panels	7	200	1400	6	200	1200	Reduce quantity
Task lights	2	200	400	1	200	200	Reduce quantity
Total			5850			4750	
Furnishings							
Carpet	120 USF*	3	360	100 USF*	3	300	Less space
Drapery	12 LF†	20	240	10 LF†	18	180	Qty/fabric cost
Artwork	2	500	1000	1	350	350	Reduce quantity
Plants	3	150	450	1	150	150	Reduce quantity
Accessories	1 SET‡	250	250	1 SET‡	175	175	No pen set
Total			2300			1155	
Summary							
Totals			8150			5905	
Sales tax	8 PERCENT		652			472	
Grand totals			8802			6377	
Cost per USF			73			64	
Projected savings							
Workstation	$2425 (27.55 percent reduction)						
Space	20 USF (16.66 percent)			$9 per USF			

*USF = usable square feet.
†LF = linear feet.
‡SET = see table 2-5.

TABLE 2.4   Potential 5-Year Furniture and Furnishings Savings for Yourco, Inc.

Cost per usable square feet		
Current standards:	$73	
New standards:	$64	
Savings per usable square foot	$9	
First year's potential saves		
Rentable square feet (000s)		517.5
Conversion to usable square feet (conversion factor of 25 percent):		388.1
First year's potential savings:	$9 × 388.1	= $3,492,900
Average save over 5 years	$3492.90 × 5 years = $17,464,500	

seniormost officer in each division be designated to approve departmental exceptions. The president or chief executive officer has no particular reason to review minimal variations. Let the division settle it.

2.3 Standards as a Design Tool

The use of standards as a design tool immediately brings to mind the sensitivity one can create by recommending a particular manufacturer or color scheme.

After all the years that I criticized bad designs and complimented good ones, I don't think this is the time to explain color concepts or schemes because it is filled with too many variables and is subject to personal tastes.

In *The World Book Dictionary,* the term "design" is defined as: "a drawing, plan, or sketch made to serve as a pattern from which to work." The word "pattern" in the definition highlights the need for the facility manager to resolve the basic design criteria:

- Open and closed space plan utilization
- Furniture systems' attributes
- Appropriateness of office furnishings.

The suggested solution becomes the pattern for usage throughout the office space. The facility manager should be addressing the number one issue in space design: flexibility. Whether the office will be an open or closed plan, the need to plan an aesthetic pattern for future changes is essential.

Open space plan

In the open plan office, the designer has several solutions available to create separate areas and patterns for offices.

The most common divider is the panel. The panels are usually fabric-covered. Additional ways to subdivide offices include storage "walls" (composed of cabinets, files, or a combination thereof), and plants and plantings.

The designer must plan on flexibility within the workstation. After all, today's employee may change tomorrow, or the function may change. The design plan must account for personal comfort, allow for personalization, and provide for privacy or openness as required by the business manager.

Design tools for the open plan

- Manner of integrating panel heights
- Variation of colors and textures in the fabric selections
- Orientation of the furniture in relation to the windows or circulation paths
- Use of plantings to create separations or to add color

Using these tools properly allows for quick, less expensive changes to meet future flexibility needs for the business and less regimentation than the closed office solution.

What does the facility manager do to resolve space set aside for a business's future growth? The basic solutions include planning a space allocation and design that affords virtually no vacancy within the contiguous workspace. The vacant spaces are grouped together.

Centralized vacancy. The dangers of this pattern of fully occupied space and fully vacant space include:

- Ability of another department to "grab" the space
- Criticism of the business manager for allowing too much space
- Inability to limit growth to the area set aside
- Probable insufficiency of vacant space for growth or change
- Saving of some initial funding by not furnishing the entire vacant area (unacceptable to facility managers because senior management views any unfurnished area that sits vacant as highly wasteful)

Decentralized vacancy. The acceptable solution for approved future growth calls for distribution of the vacant workstations directly in the area of the unit that forecast the growth. This pattern has several advantages:

- Because all the furniture is purchased up front, the space looks finished and completed.
- If the growth forecasts prove accurate, future changes appear relatively transparent, and disruption to the balance of the workers should be minimal.
- Senior management deems the business manager smart for planning ahead.
- Limiting future costs to churn costs avoids allocating more funds for furniture.
- Small pockets spread throughout the space can easily accommodate uneven growth.

Closed space plan

The closed office solution normally divides spaces by full-height solid or glass partitions. For the purists reading this, there are also combinations of glass and solid. Therefore, vacant offices, set aside for future growth, are not usually as visible to the visitor as in open planning. The unoccupied space, if left unfurnished, can cause problems such as:

- The inability to get the furniture quickly when needed
- The inability to get furniture and furnishings in matching colors and finishes
- The need for the facility manager to request that new funds be allocated at the time the extra furniture must be ordered
- The "closing off this space" phenomenon, which rarely occurs in a corporation (the possession of space looms all too important for a business manager to risk possible criticism for taking too much space.)

By spreading out the vacant space for future growth the business manager:

- Prevents another department from requesting or snatching the space away.
- Distributes the plan growth evenly over the various units that forecast a need.
- Provides offices immediately available in the right spot for planned or unplanned changes.

Furniture attributes

Interestingly enough, senior managers can visualize the successful formula for work, and they can see how work should flow, how customers will want to see advertisements, and how they should handle customer accounts. However, they cannot visualize furniture. Update the old saying "One picture is worth a thousand words" to "One mock-up is worth a thousand words the facility manager can avoid in describing the system." Mock-ups create an amazing amount of pain and suffering for all concerned.

The facility manager, who may instinctively know the best furniture solution, must impartially plan, design, study, and build a mock-up of prospective systems—naturally, for at least *three* manufacturers. The facility manager now must set aside time from an otherwise busy day.

The designer, who has not allocated time for designing the mock-up or for the study, is expected to provide this extra duty for free. There is no such thing as free. The facility manager will pay for this time sooner or later.

The furniture manufacturers view this as a bid. No one pays for bids. Therefore, the facility manager unfairly expects to get this for free. I am not advocating paying for it either. I am suggesting that you avoid the process if at all possible.

The end user has to set aside sufficient time to evaluate the mock-ups and justify the selected system with a logical and cost-effective set of reasons.

The essential design pattern lies not in the selection of wood or fabric panels, or of Steelcase or Herman Miller furniture, but rather in the attributes afforded to the facility manager.

The more variety, the more choices, and the more options available, the more acceptable the final selection will appear to the user. This allows the facility manager the flexibility to solve virtually all functional requirements of any staff member. This variety is available in both open and closed furniture systems. The closed planning attributes can be recognized when reading through the list of open planning attributes that follow.

- Panels
  - Height availability
  - Width sizes
  - Thickness
  - Central core construction
  - Leveling ease and construction
  - Surface covering (fabric, wood, vinyl, etc.)

- Hanging components

- Files (box drawers, file drawers, sizes and widths)
- Work surfaces (straight edges, waterfall, sizes, computer)
- Stationery storage units
- Tackable surfaces
- Magnetic/marker boards
- Closets/coat hooks
- Freestanding components
  - Files (same as above)
  - Keyboard and other tables
  - Work surfaces (desks, tables)
  - Panels
  - Rolling bins and tubs
- System construction
  - Materials (steel, wood, particle board, laminated veneer, plastics)
  - Assembly (clips, bolts, screws, brackets, tools)
  - Panel to panel (posts, brackets, clips, bars)
  - Component to panel (bracket, clip, screw)
  - Drawer/file suspension (ball bearings, rollers, plastic glides, nylon glides)
  - Corners (square, rounded, joint reveal, mitered)
- Lighting systems
  - Task lights (size, left/right switching, changes in intensity, how secured to system)
  - Ambient lights (size, approval by Underwriters Laboratories)
  - Other work surface lighting available
- Wiring distribution
  - Horizontal raceways at base
  - Horizontal distribution and access at work surface
  - Horizontal raceway at top of panel
  - Through-base connections
  - Vertical connections
- Maintenance
  - Ease of cleaning panels, work surfaces
  - Resistance to marring, scratches, tears
  - Ease to replace in the field
  - Damage to carpeting
- Acoustics
  - Material used in panels (fiberglass, honeycomb, polyfoam, steel)
  - Sound transmission ratings for wall systems
  - Sound absorption rating
  - Other available components (open plan closet to house word processing equipment, acoustical hoods)

- Fire and safety
  - Conformance to various national codes for fire retardancy
  - Fire spread rating
  - Fire load analysis
  - Conformance to BIFMA (Business Industrial Furniture Manufacturer's Association) and local codes
- Aesthetic appeal
  - Do you like the system?
  - Is it really functional?
  - Are the colors and finishes acceptable?
  - Are flexibility needs for your corporation met?

Office furnishings

Carpeting. Furnishings are those items other than furniture that round out the office space. The most visible furnishing, carpeting, is considered a construction item in some corporations and a furniture item in others.

While carpeting serves as an acoustical aid, it is mainly installed for comfort and aesthetic reasons. The broadloom solution is a common one. This method has been around for a long time. Unfortunately, this method does not afford the facility manager the flexibility required in making office changes.

In the old broadloom days, an office change required the following sequence (I call it the Broadloom Churn Project). See if you can calculate the costs of the various laborers to sit around while each performed a piece of the action for installing one electrical and one telephone outlet!

- Furniture mover relocates all furniture in the area.
- Carpet contractor rolls back the broadloom.
- Contractor drills new hole in floor for both an electrical outlet and a telephone outlet.
- Electrician pulls wiring.
- Telephone laborer pulls wiring.
- Carpet contractor rolls back broadloom, slices carpet for wires.
- Electrician pulls wires through hole, wires outlet.
- Telephone laborer pulls wires through hole, wires outlet.
- Mover puts all furniture back in place.
- Telephone laborer wires through desk to work surface.

The facility manager supervises the various tradespeople and stands there adding up the costs for this minor change.

Since the advent of carpet tile, modern thinking, and a change in attitude on the part of the electricians, the process (the Carpet Tile Project) runs something like this:

- Electrician drills hole through carpet tile and floor, moves one desk aside if necessary.
- Electrician pulls both electric and telephone wire.
- Electrician wires both outlets.
- Electrician shoves desk back.

The absent facility manager can be running another larger churn project elsewhere. The costs become manageable. Carpet tiles also offer instant cleaning: Throw out the soiled one and replace with a surplus one or exchange with one from under the file cabinet!

Window treatments.   There are many alternatives to shield the office from heat and sunlight. The cost and aesthetics of each option are not discussed. It is interesting to note the infighting in corporations for number of windows, which then get covered. This fact is similar to the argument for a "door in my office" versus the philosophy "my door is always open."

Among the many solutions to cover the windows are:

- Draperies (building standard, overdrapes, lacy, opaque, sheer)
- Blinds (venetian blinds that run horizontally or vertically, regular width or miniblinds, exposed to the office or between two sheets of glass)
- Shades (opaque, sunscreen, roll-down)
- Plastic sunscreen that adheres to inside face of exterior glass
- Nothing

Plants.   Plastic plants are for plastic companies. The real greenery is soothing to employees and is something that should be encouraged. Along with this furnishing is the ability to keep plants alive. A suggested solution is to have on-staff or consultant horticultural specialists. Their duties are cleaning, pruning, watering, and general maintenance.

Plants can be distributed as a standard. The facility manager can plan on the basis of cost, size, or type of plants according to rank or function. Additionally, the planter can increase in status from plastic to wood or stone as required through the ranks. The designer should plan for proper location and lighting of plants. It is important to discourage staff from relocating plants. Plants brought from home by employees may or may not be encouraged as the facility manager feels is appropriate. If it is encouraged, then the employees should be told to maintain their own plants.

Artwork.   Artwork requires careful planning and execution. The facility manager is encouraged to have the art administrator or resident expert review each plan for proper placement. If staff members are unavailable, then the facility manager should have an external consultant perform this service. Many interior design firms will do this as an extra service.

In closed planning, it is rather easy to set a standard of artwork size or range of dollar amount to be expended by each rank or level. Each closed office will virtually have the choice of two or three walls on which to hang the artwork.

In an open plan, it makes little sense to hang artwork on a panel that is 48 inches high. I suggested that the same budget be allocated. However, instead of a series of small decorative posters, use the same funds to purchase significant artwork that may be hung on corridor walls for all to enjoy. If this is not acceptable, then the corporation will end up with $50 posters inside $100 frames.

Artwork is not limited to paintings. It also includes drawings, tapestries, sculptures, and mobiles. Artwork can be purchased through galleries or museums, directly from the artist, or at auctions.

Desk accessories.   The standards for desk accessories are a small but essential part of the office. The designer is lavish with the office touches for the senior manager and spends a minimal amount of time ordering ballpoint pens for the lowest levels.

The program for standards should set a quality and quantity mark by function or rank as appropriate for the corporation. In addition to certain items not being made available to the lower rank, the quality level of the desk accessory diminishes. A suggested list of accessories that different levels of staff would get is outlined in Table 2.5.

2.4   Setting the Standards

One common factor found in many corporate programs is a very tightly controlled and structured standard allocation. This includes an

TABLE 2.5   Desk Accessory Guidelines

	Yourco, Inc., management levels				
Item	Senior	Upper	Middle	Lower	Clerical
Desk pad	Yes	Yes	Yes	Yes	No
Pen set	Double	Double	Single	Single	*
Calendar pad	Yes	Yes	Yes	Yes	No
Letter tray	Two	Two	Two	Two	*
Ashtrays†	Six	Three	One	One	One
Wastebasket	Two	One	One	One	One
Desk lamp	One	One	No	No	No
Letter opener	One	One	No	No	*
Scissors	One	One	*	*	*
Quality level	Stone	Leather	Chrome	Stainless	Plastic

*Indicates item to be ordered through Yourco, Inc., stationery, as required.
†Let's enforce no smoking and save on the ashtray expense!

allocation of color schemes, finishes, and exact sizes or shapes of offices by rank.

The facility manager should not be a police officer or a traffic enforcement agent. Facility managers should be the legislative body that creates, oversees, and coordinates an equitable broad standards outline. The facility manager should then be capable of having everyone live within the boundaries of this legislation. This "law" should be one that a corporate law-abiding individual can live within and not have to try to avoid.

The deviation process and relief from standards from within an organization makes the standards a living document. These are discussed in this section.

The common base on which standards are written is the concept of "flexibility."

Space, furniture, and construction standards must stand a test more severe than any individual manager's lack of tact in relating their opinion of adhering to standards. Standards must stand up in the fourth dimension: They must withstand the test of time.

Open plan versus closed plan

Open plan or closed plan—what is the best solution for your corporation? While this was a burning issue a few years ago, the debate really has died down in the larger corporations. The fight may still be going on in smaller companies.

The flexible office solution has to be open plan furniture and furniture systems. The use of systems affords the facility manager the most options, componentry, and arrangements to meet most employee functions.

Why would any corporation object to an open plan installation with these attributes? The initial reason may be costs. The system's solution may be more expensive at first pass. However, a view of the long-range return on the investment based on a rate of change or churn rate of 25 percent will quickly eliminate this concern.

The concept of policing the standards will soon lead the intelligent facility manager to realize that closed planning is also fine. The key criterion is to monitor the locations of the closed offices. The facility manager will want to locate the offices in a spot where the least amount of change will be required in future years.

As an example, management has a propensity for the corner office. Do not fight it, create a closed office zone in the corner, along one short side of a floor, or wherever appropriate. Once this zone is established, the balance of the floor, probably 80 percent of the space, will always be done in open plan. In some cases, a multifloor unit may have one complete floor with a ring of offices around the perimeter, while the other floors will all be open plan.

This is fine, plan for it and do not fight against the odds. Save the corporation significant money by achieving the open plan in the majority of space, and even more money by fixing the closed office location and size (if at all possible). This approach, commonly called modified open planning, becomes acceptable to both management and the facility manager. Management achieves privacy, and facility managers achieve flexibility in the part of the space that will change.

The fixed offices should be sized to the function. This will further eliminate changes in the closed planning zone. Why build a middle management office if the occupant's function is that of the next level? It will be changed with the next promotion.

Space standards

In preparing space standards, the usual question from one professional to another is "How much space should be assigned to each rank or level?"

At the 1986 International Facility Management Association Conference, I gave a speech on space standards. Strange as it may be, at the end of the hour the audience realized that square footage per office was never mentioned. The reason was simply that each company has different needs, requirements, and functions. The key is the philosophy behind the standards and the ability of their flexibility to adapt to any and all corporate situations.

In short, each corporation still needs some degree of standards set to the ranking of officers. However, with careful analysis of the various functions in the company a set of standards can be established along with a "deviation range."

The "deviation range" is a factor, approximately 10 percent, that is added to either end of the median standard established for each function or rank. If the standard office allocation for the seniormost officer in a state or country is 300 square feet, then the deviation would establish the range from 270 to 330 square feet. The standards should always be stated in both square feet and square meters to cover international staff. This range allows for variances in building modules as well as in functional requirements that an individual may need. This range eliminates or reduces the facility manager's policing the 300-square-foot target.

The space standard is all-encompassing. It is applied to open and closed planning solutions, office and customer space, and domestic and international offices.

The deviation process allows that the seniormost officer in the division or group, not in the department, be allowed to approve exceptions to the standards. The responsibility for seeking approval is up to the individual who wants the exception, not to the facility manager. The critical items to be considered in standards are acoustics, furniture, behavior, and ergonomics.

Acoustical considerations for standards

The following criteria should be utilized:

Sound masking. Noise transmission in the office can be a deterrent to employee productivity. To help control noise in the open plan, a sound-masking system is recommended. Sound masking includes an artificially produced noise similar to the hum of the air-conditioning. The noise is distributed through a system of speakers usually installed above the finished ceiling. These sounds muffle noise to reduce intelligible noise transmission from one office to the next. (The standard joke is that some offices have no intelligible noise.)

In a case of a floor with all closed offices, sound masking is usually not required. The amount of plasterboard will usually be sufficient to avoid the need for the system. If extra sound baffling is required, then the plasterboard should be run up to the underside of the floor above.

In the modified office, sound masking is to be utilized throughout the space. Most private offices will have their doors left open almost continually. However, there are usually not enough offices to reduce sound transmission.

Floor covering. The era of vinyl tile appears to be over. The solution utilized most is carpeting. Initially, broadloom was preferred for a look of continuous floor covering. The carpet affords the office a soft surface to absorb some of the noise.

The recommended solution is carpet tiles. While the noise is just one problem, the broadloom can become a maintenance problem as well as being inflexible when the next renovation occurs. Additionally, with the advent of electronic mail carts, the "invisible" track quickly wears into the broadloom.

The carpet tile appears to take the weight of these machines better in terms of wear and appearance. The tile can also be changed easily when worn or soiled. Milliken is probably the largest manufacturer of carpet tiles. Other excellent firms are Interface and Bigelow.

There are carpet tiles specifically made for high-soil and high-static areas. However, it may be cost-effective to install vinyl composite tile in these spaces.

Ceiling tile.   Noise tends to bounce off the ceiling. The better the absorption rate of the ceiling tile, the less noise will be transmitted to the next office. A minimum rating is a noise reduction coefficient (NRC) of 0.65 for the ceiling tile, with 1.00 as the optimum. Noise can be further reduced with sound baffles above the ceiling.

Equipment noise pollution.   Noise from everyday office equipment can be extremely distracting. Every word processor printer should be within an acoustical hood or cover. Each typewriter should be on a sound-absorbing pad. If this is not available, try a single carpet tile. Each piece of office equipment should be located where it may have the least impact in terms of noise pollution without losing sight of its functionality.

Furniture considerations for standards

The following criteria should be utilized:

Functionality.   The furniture should be able to solve the functions of the unit for which it is purchased. When this function goes away, the same system should be adaptable for use by the new function. Most systems offer many different components that can be used to solve functional needs.

Systems furniture will be subjected to constant use and abuse by employees. Additionally, the facility manager will be moving the furniture, adding and deleting components, moving the components up and down, wiring and rewiring throughout the raceway, and assembling and disassembling.

Most facility managers rely on the manufacturer's warranty to cover any nonabuse failures. It is interesting to note that many manufacturers have guaranteed their products for only 1 to 3 years. When negotiating national contracts, no less than 5 years is acceptable. After all, most corporations are depreciating the furniture over a 7- to 10-year period.

Brand names. By having one furniture system, the facility manager has complete flexibility in relocating departments or individuals. The establishment of a single standard also eliminates any competition among departments for the best, fanciest, or costliest furniture.

For the larger corporation, a single standard may be too difficult to accomplish. Some foreign countries simply forbid the importing of furniture or impose tariffs that make it too expensive. Additionally, in large companies, there is more chance that specialty functions cannot be solved with a single furniture system.

A single furniture system can be counterproductive, with a monotony of sameness throughtout the company. The lack of variation can be downright boring. Additionally, the facility managers run the risk of putting all their reliance on one vendor. This creates dependency on a single vendor's production schedule and pricing.

The multifurniture solution allows the facility manager to create variance from floor to floor or from one building to another. The choice of more than one system also keeps the manufacturer's pricing competitive.

The largest manufacturer of open plan furniture is Steelcase Furniture, Grand Rapids, Michigan. This company offers systems made entirely of steel, steel and wood, and now all wood. Its principal line is Steelcase 9000. The new product line is due to be released in late 1988 for 1989 delivery. These systems are durable and are used by facility managers to solve all levels of management needs.

The second largest manufacturer is Herman Miller, Zeeland, Michigan. Miller offers systems made of steel and wood, and wood and plastic. Its newest lines include Ethospace, introduced in 1985, and Action Office Encore, introduced in 1987. Ethospace offers greater flexibility, including interchangeable tiles that can instantly transform an office's look. The Action Office line is widely utilized throughout corporate general office space.

Other recognized furniture systems manufacturers include Knoll (Morrison system, introduced in 1987), Haworth, Westinghouse, Kimball-Artec, Allsteel, and over a hundred more.

The best system is the one that works best for the corporate needs. While one system works well in an advertising company, a financial institution or an electronics company may require different solutions.

Availability. The facility manager wants a system that is flexible, has great color and fabric finishes, and can actually be delivered on time!

Every manufacturer has a quick ship/rapid response/respond/rush system. However, most of these are limited offerings of colors, finishes, and products. The predominant purchases will be from standard delivery products.

Normally, an 8- to 12-week delivery time will suffice since construction will take that long to prepare the space to be furnished. Selecting a system that is available only every 20 weeks is not recommended.

The system has to be serviced in virtually every site where your corporation is located. While a dealer in the corporate "hometown" can install the selected systems furniture in other locations, it may not be to the facility manager's advantage.

Corporations want to be good neighbors in the new location. This includes, where possible, utilizing local firms. In the case of furniture, after the initial installation, using the local dealer to service the installation will be far more advantageous.

The best solution seems to be to use the dealer with which the facility manager is familiar. This dealership can manage the installation as a network dealer. The fees for installation should be prenegotiated with the manufacturer and with the two dealers involved.

The more your corporation expands domestically, the more reason to have a furniture company that not only can serve the facility manager nationally but also can offer national pricing and installation.

Wire management.   There will undoubtedly be numerous electrical and telecommunication wires that need to end up on or near the desktop of the workstation. The various methods for delivering these wires all are utilized, depending upon the building conditions and cost considerations. Regardless of the system selected, a wire plan to track office automation is important. The wire plan facilitates repairs, relocations of equipment, and interconnectivity (local area network) of technology.

Power poles.   The solution with the lowest aesthetic appeal is the power pole. This is a slim pole, about 1 ½ inches square, that runs from floor to ceiling. The wires are run from the ceiling down the inside of the pole to deliver power or telecommunications to the desktop.

The poles may have the power outlet at virtually any point along their length. This solution is normally used when no underfloor duct system exists for running the wires. The worst nightmare for the facility manager is trying to accomplish a renovation with a forest of inflexible power poles.

The wiring can be run down the columns near to which a desk is to be located. Some buildings are "column-free," which of course eliminates this alternative.

Underfloor ducts. This solution is widely utilized in buildings. The duct is a hollow tube which is installed prior to the concrete's being poured during the initial construction of the facility. In older buildings, the ducts are normally too narrow or small to satisfactorily run large amounts of wiring. The buildings with larger ducts rely on the facility manager to assure that previous wiring is removed prior to running new lines. Most of these systems have predetermined outlets that are accessed by drilling through a few inches of the concrete. Unfortunately, total flexibility is harder to achieve since the outlets may not fall where needed. This can be overcome by routing a path through the concrete back to the duct. This becomes a very costly method of restoring flexibility.

Wire molding. This solution can be utilized when the underfloor duct is not available. The wires may be run from the ceiling down a power pole or column or poked through from the floor below. The wires run along the floor with a rubber molding over them. This is highly unacceptable because it can become a tripping nuisance. The molding can get in the way of rolling carts and can interfere with furniture legs or panels.

Flat wiring. This method involves running a thin, flat ribbon of electrical wiring from a building core location to each site where power is required. The wire must be used under carpet tile because of the need to gain access to any part of the wiring during a renovation. The types of flat wiring currently available do not accommodate every type of wiring need, but they're coming. The problems with flat wiring methods include the buildup of height under the carpet tile, the need to expose excessive wiring during renovations, and the limited electrical and telecommunications wires that can be used.

Poke-through. Newer buildings may not have underfloor duct systems, so running wiring in the ceiling becomes necessary. The power pole is unacceptable, but "poke-through" avoids the problem by using the ceiling *below* the floor to be wired. This allows the facility manager to literally poke through the floor slab at almost any point where the power or telecommunication wires are required. Obviously, this cannot be done where a steel beam is located. Some poured concrete buildings will require a structural examination to assure that the structural integrity of the floor is not compromised.

The major negative aspect of this method is that the facility manager must disrupt the floor below whenever any wiring changes occur. This can be costly since the floor below will usually not permit changes during normal hours. This almost guarantees overtime installations. An additional problem occurs when the floor below is occupied by another tenant. This will require advance approval from the tenant.

Raised flooring.   This method involves the installation of a floor system that consists of square tiles. These tiles are either all steel or concrete-filled for stability and strength. The tiles are normally 24 inches square and are supported by a post system. The post can hold the corners of four tiles.

The minimum height that a floor is raised is usually 4 to 6 inches. The flooring is raised 12 to 18 inches in a data center owing to the excessive wiring. Under the raised floor, wiring can be mounted on top of the finished floor. There are no restrictions on routing the wires from one point to another. The wires can then come through cutouts in the tile.

In more sophisticated uses, the wires are tethered from a box mounted on the finished floor below the raised floor to a box mounted to the underside of the floor tile. This allows the facility manager to literally relocate electrical and telephone wiring by lifting the tile and moving it to another location within the limitations of the tether. And no electricians will be required!

This method affords the facility manager the most ease of renovation and unlimited flexibility. However, to retrofit raised flooring into an existing building may require excessive ramping from the building core elements, such as the elevator lobbies and bathrooms. Furthermore, the height may result in a raised-floor-to-ceiling height that is uncomfortable.

Furniture raceways.   The manufacturers have come up with their own versions of wire management. The systems furniture have evolved from virtually no room to run wiring to some very flexible wiring systems.

The panels used to enclose workstations and provide support for hung componentry also do double duty by carrying the wiring. The first location that can be used for running wires is the entire base of the panel. This usually consists of easily removable plates that run the entire width of the panel. The initial connection into the raceway must be from one of the other wiring methods outlined above. Depending upon local codes, several workstations, with many outlets per workstation, can be wired through one base connection. The panels also have vertical spaces that allow the wires to come up from the raceway to desk height. In a way, the power pole solution is buried within the confines of the panel.

Some of the newer systems, such as Ethospace, offer a raceway or beltway at desk height. Other manufacturers offer yet another raceway at the top of the panel. The result of all these raceways is almost unlimited space to run any and all wires among workstations. These raceways enable the facility manager to make wiring changes with less work.

Some negative aspects include the extra costs to install and disassemble these raceways in certain areas where labor unions have strangleholds on electrical installations. New York City, Chicago, and Los Angeles are among these hot-spot regions.

Behavioral considerations for standards

The following criteria should be utilized:

Human factors.   Each employee needs to have a sense of place and personal territory. With closed planning, this is easily achieved by personalization within the individual office. Allowing such personalization below the height of the open plan panels is recommended.

Each employee can use the tackable or magnetic surfaces within the workstation for personal photos or other memorabilia. Management should discourage items that stick up above the panel height, which tend to be eyesores.

The sense of team relationships or privacy can be achieved through well-planned circulation patterns. In the case of teams, the access to several workstations would open on a common entry. Privacy can be achieved by separate distinct entrances to each workstation.

Personalization allows employees to take their items with them easily when relocated. It is not recommended to change color schemes or office sizes because of the whims of the incumbent employee. This becomes costly to install initially and is guaranteed to be changed with the next employee.

Management practices.   Employees usually take pride in their own space. However, the manager must encourage and reinforce this attitude. The business manager should constantly be aware of continuing maintenance and appearance issues within a space.

It is usually not possible for the facility manager to be on every floor every day. The facility manager relies upon the manager to be the eyes and ears for maintenance items.

Some of the daily items include bulb burnouts, scratch marks on the walls or panels, carpet stains, missing ceiling tiles, general housekeeping, plumbing problems, loose or exposed wires, or damaged furniture.

Ergonomic considerations for standards

The World Book Dictionary published by *The World Book Encyclopedia* defines "ergonomics" as "the study of the relationship between individuals and their work or working environment...the essential nature of ergonomics is the convergence of the disciplines of human biology (especially anatomy, physiology, and psychology) on the problems of Man at work."

The ergonomic considerations fall into the following general areas of concern: management practices, workspace (office), workplace (workstation), equipment (machinery and video display units, known as VDUs), and the associated keyboard.

Management practices. Both business managers and facility managers must incorporate ergonomic criteria into planning, designing, and constructing the workplace. The business manager lends support and financial approval for ergonomic solutions. The facility manager must assure that all areas of concern are covered.

The properly installed workplace and workstation will lead to a more productive staff. Management must ensure that each employee is properly trained in the use of all equipment and furniture that will be used in the workspace. This includes those employees on night shifts. Management must ensure that newly hired employees are also properly trained prior to actually starting on the job.

When new equipment is introduced, employees should be trained in advance. It is also recommended that the training officer be available during the first few days of the actual use of the new equipment.

From time to time, management should offer a refresher course on existing equipment to ensure that employees are utilizing it correctly and in a cost-effective manner.

Workspace (office). In addition to acoustical considerations outlined in this chapter, the following ergonomic concerns must be addressed:

Proper lighting. The ideal goal is to have nonglare ceiling fixtures and a light level at the work surface that is conducive to the task to be performed. The nonglare fixtures ensure little or no reflectivity on VDU screens or on the work surface itself.

The work surface should be one that does not reflect light. The light level at the work surface should be at least 50 footcandles (530 lux) without glare or shadow.

Furniture systems offer task and ambient lighting. A task light is usually mounted under the upper storage cabinet of a furniture system. This places a light source directly over the work surface. The ambient light would be placed on top of the upper storage unit. The light is bounced off the ceiling and reflected downward.

There are no light fixtures in the ceiling. This indirect lighting creates a warmer look but requires careful engineering to avoid dark areas and to ensure an even distribution of light.

Ventilation. Adequate ventilation includes the delivery of heat and air-conditioning to all workstations in a balanced way. This means that areas with extra equipment, for example, will usually require increased air-conditioning and less heating. Additionally, the removal of foul air and equipment-generated heat and/or fumes must be properly engineered.

The proper, comfortable temperature and humidity must be maintained throughout the workspace. This includes the assurance that the workspace is comfortable on the first day of the workweek. Productivity can be reduced dramatically on a hot day in the summer when the air-conditioning is not working.

Ventilation also includes the maintenance of heating, ventilation, and air-conditioning (HVAC) mechanical equipment, ductwork, and filters.

Workplace (workstation). The furniture system utilized should be flexible to accommodate changes in work surface height as required. The system should allow for extra componentry to be added or removed with minimal disruption to the workstation itself. The best solution would be to use panel systems that are designed to accommodate components to be clipped onto the panel on 1-inch centers.

The chair should provide the employee with proper back support for the function. An additional goal would be to have the back cushion adjustable since each employee requires a different height. It is also recommended that the seat height be adjustable for the same reason. This adjustability is all-important in multishift operations because the chair will be used by two or three different employees each day.

Data centers, mail rooms, and truck dock dispatching stations are areas where employees are required to stand most of the workday. It is recommended that a padded rubber mat with beveled edges be provided. The beveled edge eliminates tripping hazards, while the rubber is nonconductive.

If it is required, the employee should have a footrest and/or an armrest available. The facility manager should ensure that windows are covered with shades, blinds, or some other window treatment. Facility managers should try to eliminate any wire clutter on the desk surface as well as below it.

Equipment (machinery and VDUs). Heavy-duty machinery should have proper safeguards against employee injuries to fingers, hands, and eyes. The safety director, unit supervisor, or facility manager should ensure that the proper personal equipment, such as safety glasses, is used when necessary.

Business needs are always paramount in selecting electronic equipment. However, when more than one computer can respond to the business criteria, then the following ergonomic concerns should be addressed:

- Screen contrast between characters and background should be distinct.
- Screen should not flicker.
- Characters should be large and readable.
- Screen should be nonglare or contain a hood to shield the screen from overhead light.
- VDU should have controls to adjust contrast and brightness.
- VDU should be movable (up/down, left/right).
- VDU should be made of antireflective material.
- VDU controls should be easily accessible.
- VDU base should be as small as possible to allow more work surface to be available for employee papers.

Keyboard. The keyboard should be separate from the VDU. This allows each employee to place the keyboard in the most comfortable position and angle. The keyboard should be lightweight and easily manipulated.

When heavy numerical tasks are performed, a keypad calculator should be built into the keyboard. Furniture systems also offer articulated keyboards and drawers. A drawer literally is installed under the work surface and the keyboard is placed inside. The employee slides the drawer out when the keyboard is in use, and, when finished, the employee slides the drawer back out of the way.

2.5 The Words of Others—Standards: Setting and Selling

Neville Lewis   *President, P.H.H. Neville Lewis*

Put simply, "standards" are a rational way to approach the complexities of interior environments. A sense of order and direction is a tool (or crutch) to be used to face the immediate bureaucracy that interior planning and the selection of furnishings can create.

In the hedonistic society which exists today—with the strenuous competition for personnel added to the fact that interior costs are rising faster than exterior construction costs—we must have a system to allow for rational choice.

In reality, large companies or institutions cannot effectively plan without consistent standards for both planning and furnishings. The important thing to remember is that any standard must have some flexibility so that variations can be achieved and some chance of individual statement can be made. Too rigid a standard can make a space "prisonlike," and the long-range effect can be a lack of user productivity.

Many designers and or facility managers forget that human beings will occupy the spaces they plan. The result of this forgetfulness is a space that does not work, and while it solves logistics, it does not deal with the human condition.

When a designer meets with a new client and is told that "we have a standards program," there is an initial fear that there is no room for creativity. In some cases this is correct since the selections and standards are in many cases outmoded and have not grown along with the company. The lesson here is that standards have to be reevaluated so that they are constantly responding to growth and technology.

As with everything else, knowing when to stop and understanding the user need, plus a certain elasticity in approach, should ensure that standards control the environment and user needs control the standards.

3

Project Management: An Approach

3.1 Introduction

Remember the good old days? Realtors offered space to let. Architectural firms did architecture. Interior design firms did interior design. Engineering firms did engineering. Construction firms did construction. Furniture manufacturers manufactured furniture. Furniture dealers installed and serviced furniture. This was prior to this phenomenon called Facility or Project Management. And it was only in 1980. What happened?

In the old days corporate users were subject to competition only within each of several disciplines listed above. A truly coordinated churn or renovation was hard to achieve. Each of these disciplines walked away at the end of the job, unconcerned with the corporation's ability to make the space work or to handle the day-to-day changes.

Project management approach

Corporations, desperate to control the process, initially sought out the architectural firms to manage the process. The architects were "above" handling mundane, routine types of work and avoided the call to duty. Corporations turned to their in-house staff and suddenly embraced the concept of *facility management*.

This decision was obviously correct, otherwise this book could never have been written or read. While the various functions of facility management have always existed within a corporation, they were never subject to a team leader, the professional facility manager.

Facility management grew instantly in the larger corporations. Smaller corporations allowed their in-house staff to grow at a slower rate. Meanwhile, panic set in at the offices of the various external consultants. Dollar signs were flying by without stopping at their drafting boards. The disciplines realized that facility management was here to stay.

If you can't beat them, join them. The disciplines jumped on board the facility train. They began to expand their services. Real estate firms offered space as well as architectural and construction management services. Architectural firms reoffered architecture, interior design, and construction management. Interior design firms offered architectural services, engineering design, construction management, and furniture purchasing, in addition to interior design. Engineering firms offered all engineering services, architectural design, and construction management. Construction firms offered all design-build-construct services, which literally encompass realty, architecture, interior design, engineering, and furniture purchasing. Furniture manufacturers offered dealer services, interior design, including programming and inventorying, and, in some rare cases, they continued to manufacture furniture! Furniture dealers offered interior design, furniture purchasing, and traditional services such as installation and servicing previously installed furniture. It has gotten rough out in the consultant world.

The in-house facility manager continues to flourish and benefit by this increased competition. The rivalry for the facility business has kept the prices sharp and the services excellent, and there is concern by the disciplines for the day-to-day success of their services to the corporation.

In 1988 the firms have learned their lesson well. The trend is for these firms to offer facility management services to the corporation. This could become interesting since the corporation may have an opportunity to retain in their employ fewer staff members, but those will be quality individuals.

Corporations will utilize more consultant services to fill the void. Displaced facility professionals will end up in the consultant sector servicing their former employers. All the disciplines are now on board the facility management train.

Locomotive	Facility managers
Sleeper	Realtors
Passenger	Architects
Smoker	Interior designers
Coal car	Engineers
Freight	Construction firms
Hopper	Furniture manufacturers
Caboose	Furniture dealers

Unfortunately, it seems that everyone is crowded into the locomotive trying to be all things for the facility manager. The facility manager is trying to lead the way to the end of the project line. Someone has to get off at the next stop. The corporation does not want the facility manager to detrain. After all, the corporation does own the tracks!!

3.2 Establishing the Project Management Department

There comes a career point when the facility manager realizes that the volume of projects is such that help is needed. The corporation relies on the project manager to lead the team.

What is this team? The introduction to this chapter outlined many of the external consultants that are employed throughout the project's life cycle.

Responsibilities of the team

Many in-house staff are necessary to the success of the project. Essential staff and key responsibilities are shown below.

- Project manager
  - Overall coordination and leadership of project team
  - Overall financial control and approval
  - Status reporting
- Designer
  - Reviewing or performing all design documentation
  - Assuring conformance to corporate design, furniture, and space standards
  - Seeking cost-effective solutions without sacrificing quality
  - Coordinating with engineer
  - Financial reporting to project manager on adherence to project budgets
- Furniture buyer
  - Reviewing design in progress to assure compliance with furniture standards and availability of goods
  - Selecting appropriate firms to bid on buyer-approved specifications
  - Negotiating and awarding purchases to qualified firms
  - Issuing purchase orders, follow-up on delivery to ensure conformance with project schedule
  - Reporting financial status to project manager on adherence to project budgets

- Engineer
    - Selecting electrical systems—lighting, wiring and electrical power distribution
    - Selecting environmental systems—HVAC: heating, ventilation, and air-conditioning
    - Selecting acoustical systems—paging, sound masking
    - Selecting electrical delivery systems—underfloor ducts, power poles, raised flooring, poke-through
    - Planning for special engineering items—kitchen, materials handling, telecommunications, data centers, transportation and mail
    - Planning life safety systems
    - Planning security systems
    - Planning building management systems

- Construction manager
    - Reviewing contract documentation
    - Selecting appropriate firms to bid on documentation
    - Writing request for proposal (RFP) outlining exact project criteria
    - Negotiating and awarding contracts
    - Preparing construction schedules and budgets
    - Supervising construction in progress in the field
    - Reporting financial status to project manager on adherence to project budgets

- Financial analyst
    - Establishing financial procedures with project manager at project's origination
    - Receiving and posting approved invoices for payment
    - Preparing and reporting on project's financial status

- User Coordinator
    - Coordinating information representing the various units within the user's organization
    - Securing necessary approvals during the project's life cycle
    - Attending and representing the user at project meetings and at the move-in

While the list of responsibilities represents the initial team for a project, the facility manager must rely on many other professionals during the project's life cycle. All the above, except for the user coordinator, should be members of the in-house facility team. Owing to corporate restraints on facility budgets, it is quite acceptable to utilize the world of external consultants.

The recommended interviewing and pricing tactics appear in Chapter 5. However, most facility managers seem to have the impression that consultants are evil. It is amazing that professional corporate facility managers fail to remember that "except for the grace of the CEO (chief executive officer) there goes *us*." There are distinct differences in thinking when one is employed within a corporation as opposed to a consulting firm. However, the functions do remain the same.

Staffing

The external consultants should be considered members of the team and not held in an adverserial position. Their prices are still negotiated, and they do not escape criticism for failures or oversights. They are performing an extension of the facility manager's job that cannot be done in-house owing to limited staffing availability. The facility manager with a limited budget for in-house staff should concentrate on maintaining a quality corporate staff to manage and understand the work of the external consultants.

Project manager.   At a minimum, the project management should always be performed by a corporate employee. The level of financial and corporate responsibilities requires an in-house staff employee to oversee all aspects of the project.

Interior designer.   The interior design is dependent on the type and quantity of work to be performed. Small renovation projects can be covered with minimal in-house staff. During peak periods of churn work, external consultants can always be brought in to fill the void. New building construction almost always requires the use of external consultants. The reasons include the following:

- Consultants have a familiarity with local conditions.
- There is always a need to file with local authorities.
- A massive amount of drafting (electronic or manual) for a complete set of drawings is required.
- Full-time dedication to the project required is not always available to in-house staff because of changing corporate priorities.

Engineer.   The engineering staffing is similar to that of the interior designer for the same reasons. While most facility managers have strong design backgrounds, they may not have equally strong engineering experience. If this is the case, then it is recommended that an in-house engineer with mechanical and electrical background be employed.

Purchasing manager. Furniture buying should be accomplished in-house all the time. The specifications portion of the project can always be performed by external designers.

The purchasing power with the manufacturer is best when exercised from within the company. Additionally, the larger corporations will almost always receive better discounts from vendors than the design firms will receive. Chapter 6 explores this purchasing clout.

The purchasing function should *not* be part of another unit in the corporation because a very close working relationship is essential during the critical periods of a project. The buyer, when needed to manage the project purchases, should not report elsewhere in the company and be subjected to priorities of purchasing equipment or pencils.

Construction manager. The construction department size should be dependent upon volume as well. At a minimum, a construction manager should be in-house to manage and supervise the various construction trades. Very large construction projects will undoubtedly require utilizing a construction firm. The determinant is always the time and staffing needs.

Additional problems in certain areas involve corporate concerns about unions. Major companies employ very few laborers and will rely on local firms to supply the required help. Some companies will keep a small staff in-house to perform churn work, including minor electrical and telephone outlet changes.

The foregoing presented major responsibilities and roles. The next section outlines the various activities during the project, with suggested staffing needs for each phase. This aid can be from professionals within the corporation or from external consultants.

Organizing the facility project

The outline of project steps may be expanded or condensed, depending on size and complexity. The sample below assumes a need to relocate an existing business that is expanding into a new location. Therefore, a new site with either a new building or a move into an existing building would be required. A move from one floor to another floor still requires many of these steps.

The facility manager's project reporting is required on a regular basis; it is not shown but is understood to be consistent throughout the project. Each discipline will supply financial information. This information is coupled with timing and other critical data in a project report produced on a regular basis.

Project phases

The project goes through six phases. Although there may be disagreement on the exact number of phases, the number of steps and the process are all the same. In this text, the six general phases of a project are as follows:

- Feasibility, programming, and requirement gathering phase.
  - Write the business plan.
  - Put together the facilities team.
  - Review sites for relocations.
  - Define technological requirements.
- Real property services phase.
  - Identify and analyze sites for new buildings or for leasing space.
  - Review the pros and cons of leasing versus owning, especially to include rent, taxes, operating cost escalations, depreciation, cost to finance the relocation, and write-off of discarded furniture and construction items.
- Approvals phase.
  - Obtain the proper approvals—the most important phase. Without the approvals, the project ends at this phase.
- Design and engineering development phase.
  - Design, engineer, and complete all drawings and documentation to be utilized in the implementation phase.
- Implementation phase.
  - Send out design documents to qualified firms to solicit prices.
  - Proceed with construction and furniture installation to accomplish the relocation.
- Postoccupancy phase.
  - Close out the project financially.
  - Verify that all installed equipment is working.
  - Poll the employees' opinion on the relocation by conducting a postoccupancy evaluation.
  - Prepare to churn the new facility as part of the daily facility process.

During each of these phases, the facility manager may be utilizing in-house and external consultants. The following table is a suggested list of the detailed steps in each of the phases and the appropriate personnel to use:

What	Who	How
Business Plan		
Define the overall business, market, and strategic plans.	Business manager, financial staff, facility manager	In-house staff only
Location Requirements		
Interpret business plans to determine minimum site and location requirements.	Facility manager, real property manager, business manager	In-house staff only
Technology		
Determine telecommunications (voice and data transmission), electrical, and other utility needs.	Facility manager, engineers	In-house facility manager, in-house and/or external engineers
Real Property		
Identify, review, inspect, and analyze sites, properties, or buildings to meet business, technical and locational needs. Make financial comparisons of viable selections.	Real estate brokers, real estate manager, facility manager, financial analyst, architect, engineers	External brokers, architect, and engineer; in-house facility manager, real estate manager, and financial analyst; architect and engineer if possible
Approvals		
Obtain corporate approvals on either purchase or lease of identified site via a preliminary document that requests funding.	Facility manager, financial analyst, business manager	All in-house staff; the facility manager must approve virtually every additional step. The facility manager secures the appropriate level of management approvals from the user coordinator through the business manager and senior manager. This approval process is not shown each time but is essential.
Building Design		
Complete architectural plans: structural, mechanical, electrical, plumbing, civil, life safety, telecommunications.	Architects, engineers, facility manager, business manager	Architects and engineers, external; balance, in-house
Master Planning		
Identify all departments to be relocated to new site.	Facility manager, space planner	In-house only, if possible

What	Who	How
	Stacking Plan	
Assign particular floors within building to each identified proposed occupant.	Facility manager, space planner	In-house only if possible
	Scheduling	
Track all activities.	Scheduler (sometimes performed by facility manager)	In-house
	Interior Design	
Complete feasibility studies, block allocations, developmental designs, contract documents (see Chapter 5).	Interior designers, facility manager	In-house design if possible
	Special Services	
Complete plans for landscape architecture and lighting, acoustical, kitchen, security, and health and medical services.	Facility manager and experts in each required speciality area	Usually a corporation does not have this extensive staffing and external consultants will be required.
	Request for Proposals	
Prepare a written outline of construction needs, scheduling and project descriptions and send to qualified construction firms for pricing.	Facility manager, construction manager	In-house, usually
	Bidding	
Solicit bids for furniture, telecommunications equipment, etc. Analyze bids, conduct negotiations, and award contracts.	Facility manager, furniture buyer, engineer, financial analyst	In-house
	Contracts	
Prepare agreements with each trade or discipline.	Facility manager, construction manager, lawyers	In-house staff and external consultants
	Construction	
Complete physical construction of office building or space.	Facility manager, construction manager, contractors, architects, interior designers, engineers	Require all appropriate participants to monitor, supervise, or oversee work.

What	Who	How
Telecommunications		
Plan, design, purchase, install all voice and data communications lines and equipment.	Facility manager, engineer	Usually external consultants
Furniture		
Track all purchased furniture, carpeting, signage, furnishings through order acknowledgment, production, and delivery, and installation.	Facility manager, furniture buyer, interior designer	In-house and external consultants
Punchlist		
Walk through project installation *prior* to move-in. Have each discipline list all items that are installed improperly, missing, damaged, or that require some follow-up. This step usually bends with the pressure to move in and ends up being performed after occupancy.	Facility manager and each discipline	In-house and external consultants
Occupancy		
Complete the physical relocation of designated departments from existing locations to new facility.	Facility manager, moving firm, equipment vendors, user coordinators (move captains)	In-house coordinators and external movers and vendors
Postoccupancy		
Evaluate employee satisfaction with relocation, verify mechanical and equipment warranties, receipt of outstanding invoices, and financial closing of project.	Facility manager, financial analyst, engineers, postoccupancy specialists	In-house and external consultants
Facility Management		
Establish procedures for maintenance of all operating equipment, day-to-day follow-up on space and furniture changes required to meet normal demands of users.	Facility manager and appropriate disciplines	In-house and external consultants depending on in-house staffing

3.3   Survival in the Corporate Environment

The job requirement or position description for the facility manager should include, but doesn't, the following essential ingredients: ability to listen, common sense, logic, management experience, personality, sense of humor, stamina, tact, understanding of corporate politics.

The role of the facility manager in the corporation requires an individual with special abilities. It is important to have the qualities listed because the larger the corporation, the more unusual the circumstances one must contend with in resolving facilities issues.

An earlier chapter outlined some of the possible locations for the facilities management despartment in the organization. The facility manager may have to live within the structure of the organization. The closer the individual is to the top, the better the chances of securing senior management approval during critical situations and for corporate funding.

Career path

The career path of an individual need not start and end at the same place. The suggested career path may go something like this:

1. Junior staff designer/architect

2. Staff designer/architect

3. Senior designer/assistant project manager

4. Project manager

5. Senior project manager

6. Senior project manager, line operations or department manager in facilities management

7. Chief of staff, line operations head or corporate officer in facilities management

8. Senior management position

While one path grows within the facilities department, another can lead to line responsibilities that include other than facility operations. On the other hand, if the pressures of the job get to be too much, try another career. Hard work, paying attention to details, and awareness of oneself within the corporate environment can lead either up or nowhere!

It is always important to have a senior manager who is looking out for you. If the facility manager is caught between two senior managers who vary in their goals, then unemployment is close at hand. It is difficult, perhaps impossible, to answer to conflicting supervisors.

Other management books point out that it is better to pull than push. This means if you have to go to bat for yourself all the time, you will not be as successful as the person who has a senior manager doing the promoting.

The facility manager who is smarter than the next person is the one who will succeed. Never play both ends against the middle in a large corporation. Always resolve conflicts individually, and do not try to tie two situations together that do not belong together.

Perhaps "resourcefulness" should be added to the position requirements.

A business manager would not expect the facility manager to run the business, understand its customers, or hire and fire its personnel. However, every business manager is an expert in facilities management. The facility manager will quickly discover that all 20,000 employees, if asked, will have an opinion on how to run the project. Some employees do not even have to be asked. They will let their opinion be known.

As the facility manager, you need to establish your own turf. What is it that you are hired to do? The previous section outlined the various roles during the life of the project. The next section highlights as many of the responsibilities as possible that should be performed by various personnel within facilities management.

Position description: Dimensions

The captions and job responsibilities listed below should be used as points in a position description. The facility manager selects the roles performed. However, the facility manager should be defining the breadth of the job by establishing the people and financial dimensions of the job.

The dimensions of the job include the following criteria:

- Number of staff managed
  - Directly managed staff accountable to facility manager (designer, engineer, assistant facility managers)
  - Matrix managed staff accountable to another manager except in performance of a project (financial analyst who reports to the accounting unit head but to the facility manager on a project)
  - Contract staff (individuals who work for the external consultant but under the direction of the facility manager; can be a sizable number of personnel)
- Number of customers served
  - Various corporate departments, tenants within a corporation's building, or facilities work performed for corporate clients

- Location of customers, number of cities, states, countries
- Budget responsibilities
  - Total salary and benefits managed
  - Total operating expenses managed
  - Total revenues managed
- Project responsibilities
  - Dollar volume and number of capital projects
  - Dollar volume and number of expense projects
  - Amount of rentable square feet
  - Rental value of space
  - Land value of property
  - Risk assets
- Education
  - High school for lowest positions
  - Basic college for most positions
  - Advanced degree for advanced positions
- Experience
  - Under 2 years for lowest positions
  - Two to 5 years for intermediate positions
  - Five to 10 years for higher positions
  - Over 10 years for advanced positions
- Organizational reporting
  - Staff job, no direct line management responsibilities for lower-pay positions
  - Staff and line job for most facility positions that have more than just a secretary as a direct report
  - Line job, in the direct chain of command between the seniormost officer of the company and this position

Position description: Services

Listed below are captions of responsibilities that must be performed during the life cycle of a project by the facilities management department. The key personnel usually associated with the task are indicated by initial after each caption; the key to these initials is:

*F*acility manager, project or construction manager

*D*esigner or architect

*A*rt administrator

*E*ngineer

*B*uyer of furniture, furnishings, and equipment

Scheduler or secretarial assistant

1. Develop and maintain corporate master space plan.
   F

2. Manage space allocations, space inventory.
   F

3. Develop, review, and approve all corporate facility expenditures.
   F

4. Undertake financial responsibilities for all project expenditures.
   F

5. Handle project management responsibilities for all projects.
   F

6. Act as principal liaison with user departments.
   F

7. Serve as team leader for project work. Team includes architects, designers, planners, engineers, art administration, special consultants, construction contractors.
   F D A E B S

8. Review leases and new property acquisitions, including work letters.
   F D E

9. Plan and design all interior and exterior plans which include feasibility studies, programming, development of design, selection of furniture, furnishings, and equipment.
   F D A E B

10. Conduct research into new products and systems.
    F D E B

11. Increase education through attendance at seminars, expositions (and through this book).
    F D A E B S

12. Comply with and understand local building codes and zoning ordinances having jurisdiction.
    F D E

13. Prepare request for quotations to be used to hire consultants for specific functions throughout the facility project.
    F D A E B

14. Negotiate, hire, review, monitor performance, approve payment, and manage external consultants.
    F D A E B

15. Investigate potential use of specialty furniture or contractors firms, e.g., woodworking.
    F D A E B

16. Inspect manufacturer's plants to assure quality of ordered goods.
    F D E B

17. Develop, negotiate, and monitor national furniture purchasing agreements.
    F B

18. Develop programs, manage staff utilization of in-house computer-aided design system.
    F D

19. Review and specify furniture for purchase.
    F D B

20. Manage the reuse or sale of surplus furniture.
    F B

21. Perform value engineering during the life cycle of a project, which means cost reductions without loss of quality.
    F D A E B S

22. Manage art purchasing, framing, curatorial, and related art services for all projects.
    A

23. Provide urban planning for new properties.
    F D E

24. Develop, publish, and monitor corporate space, furniture, and construction standards and guidelines.
    F D A E B

25. Monitor all engineering drawings and work.
    F E

26. Review vendor acknowledgments.
    F B

27. Prepare punchlist at project's completion for missing items or work to be corrected.
    F D A E B

28. Develop training courses for staff on all departmental computers.
    F D E B

29. Purchase, monitor, and receive furniture and equipment.
    F D B

30. Perform energy consumption audits.
    F E

31. Perform environmental audit for toxicity.
   F E

32. Manage library of materials, catalogs, products.
   F D A E B

33. Manage the moving process, including user scheduling meetings, tagging, color-coding, special handling, rigging, actual move, and occupancy.
   F D B S

34. Plan, purchase, and monitor installation of corporate telecommunications equipment.
   F E

35. Advise on specification and placement of art-related items, including artwork, sculptures, tapestries, rugs, mirrored walls, custom antique pieces.
   A

36. Assign project numbers, projects, and project tracking.
   F S

37. Handle typing, scheduling of meetings, ordering supplies, travel arrangements, dictation/transcription, telephone calls, managing temporary services, maintaining files, follow-up coordination, personnel recordkeeping, and attendance.
   S

Through the years, corporate personnel or human resources staff have become better informed on facility management. They **almost** understand what to review and what to evaluate on facility position descriptions. In the past, the facility manager would attack the position description form by writing more details, more explanations, and volumes of information. It was difficult for such reviewers to comprehend the complexity and depth and breadth of services performed by staff in the facilities management department.

With the advent of comparative grading systems, such as the "Hay Point" system, the reviewer simply quantifies the dimensions of the job for a point value which is taken off a master index subscribed to by the various corporations. The next step is to assess or equate the responsibility level to other management responsibility levels and be given a point value. The sum of the points determines the level within the corporation.

Action words speak louder

Since part of the evaluation requires comparison of management levels, it is important to use key words and phrases that demonstrate control. Always use an action word to describe the activity: the facility manager is always in action but the human resources sector has to be reminded! A suggested list of action verbs and words follows.

Advise	Institute
Analyze	Insure
Arrange	Maintain
Assess	Manage
Coach	Monitor
Conduct	Operate
Control	Organize
Coordinate	Oversee
Create	Perform
Decrease	Plan
Design	Prepare
Develop	Promote
Direct	Provide
Educate	Reduce
Eliminate	Research
Establish	Review
Evaluate	Revise
Execute	Schedule
Explore	Select
Handle	Supervise
Hire	Test
Identify	Train
Implement	Update
Increase	Write
Install	

Survival of the facility manager

While writing this book, I kept a list of principal activities and items that crossed my desk over a 10-day period. Examples of the same types facing facility managers in every corporate environment are these:

1. Published a space inventory covering millions of rentable square feet.

2. Had informal handshake on 60,000 square feet in a new building for a fixed cost per square foot. Discovered the user now needs about twice as much space owing to reorganization. The same

landlord said it would be no problem but, now that he had us, *added* $1 per square foot.

3. Got a call that employees reported seeing mice on the fourth floor.

4. Finalized 5-year carpet purchasing agreement and a 5-year desk accessories agreement.

5. Received requests for 21 new projects.

6. Issued about $300,000 of purchase orders for new furniture.

7. Signed a major expenditure proposal (see explanation in budgeting section) for a new telecommunications switch that includes new instruments for 15,000 lines.

8. Had a staff meeting and listened to staff complain of on-line project tracking system's giving them more work but accurate information and better project history. They are right.

9. Promoted one staff member, gave out two raises, hired one secretary, interviewed for two more.

10. Wrote a position description for art project manager, hired someone for the position, but she had to take a drug abuse test. She tested negative (which is good). Performing the test is *not* part of my position description!

11. Took no days off.

12. Had two vendor lunches, ate at my desk once, ate the rest of the meals in our officers' dining room.

13. Stacked our new high-rise office building under construction in New York.

14. Got a call that the federal tax examiners have arrived for their unannounced audit, and they need space today.

15. The electronic doors on the chairman's floor worked flawlessly for their first nine months. Today, someone could not get them to open. You are correct; that someone was the chairman.

Summary

The fate of the facility manager is sealed from the moment the job is filled. A news release in a trade magazine stated that a manager deserves hazardous duty pay when asked to coordinate an office move—not because the relocation task can be nerve-frazzling, which it can, but because of the likely impact on his or her career.

A study found that 68 percent of the managers responsible for arranging corporate moves were either demoted or fired after the move because of foul-ups during the move or because the stressful experience produced reduced job performance.

With all you learn from this book, your survival is practically guaranteed!

3.4 Managing the Project Meetings

The facility manager serves as the team leader throughout the project's life cycle. Leadership means having responsibility for all aspects of the project, right down to having project meetings.

Facility managers without leadership abilities should be off taking a leadership course right now. Every project requires face-to-face meetings among the team members chaired by the facility manager. The rights of the facility manager as meeting leader are not written down, except in this text. It is amazing that the normal team members must be taught over and over again. The team learns to listen and cooperate over time.

Meetings and attendees

Project inception. The initial kickoff meeting—always required—brings the facility manager and the user contact together to define the scope of the project. Attendees are the facility manager, user coordinator, and designer; on larger projects you need an architect and an engineer.

Programming. The programming of key personnel ascertains detailed staff needs. This is done through questionnaires and follow-up interviews on larger projects. Smaller churn projects usually require just the interview with a form filled out at the meeting or after the meeting. Attendees are the facility manager, user coordinator, designer, and business manager. The user coordinator's presence at these meetings serves to remind the business manager that one of the business manager's staff is part of the team and available to answer questions.

Preliminary design. During the initial block allocations and design phases it is important *not* to allow the designer to meet with the user alone. The designer may not appreciate the tight time or dollar restraints on the project when suggesting an expensive fabric or long-lead item. While some designers are mindful of these restraints, they cannot relate to other disciplines being managed by the facility manager. Attendees are the facility manager, user coordinator, designer, engineer, construction manager, and furniture buyer.

Financial approvals. The overall financial project costs are forecast and budgeted during this phase. The final numbers are put together in a financial document for approval by senior management. This is outlined in Chapter 4.3. Attendees are the facility manager, designer, engineer, user coordinator, financial analyst, construction manager, and furniture buyer.

Regularly scheduled project meetings. *Frequency:* The facility manager will set a frequency rate for the regular project meeting that is commensurate with the complexity of the project and the particular phase of its life cycle. For example, meetings may be every other week through the contract documents phase, and then:

- Weekly through construction
- Twice a week during the last few weeks prior to the move
- Every other week through punchlist
- One last time at project closing

Scribe: The designer usually takes the minutes to allow the facility manager to run the meeting. Each action item should include, in separate columns, the person who is responsible and the target date for completion of the action. A secretary or other individual who is not familiar with the terms and expressions used should not be the scribe.

Agenda: The last meeting's minutes become the agenda for this meeting. At the end of the old minutes, new business items can be added. Completed items are recorded as completed and removed from the minutes after the next meeting. The minutes form a written history of the project's critical items as they occur and are resolved, which can be used to resolve future differences on responsibilities and understandings. Attendees are the facility manager, designer, engineer, user coordinator, construction manager, and furniture buyer.

Move meetings. In addition to the normal team, the move captains are invited to ensure that all parties involved with the relocation know each other. This meeting is essential to ensure that each person knows who is responsible for each item during the final move-in. Attendees are the facility manager, designer, engineer, user coordinator, construction manager, furniture buyer, and (do not forget) the *mover*.

It is best to utilize a computer to maintain minutes. Minutes are just changes to selected items in a prepared text. This makes minutes perfect for word processing software on the computer. Once the initial minutes are typed, they become easy to maintain. There is no reason for the scribe to constantly retype the minutes.

Delegation

1. The rules become simple if one remembers *The World Book Dictionary* definition of "delegate": "a person given power or authority to act for others, a representative." The facility manager is responsible for the project's overall financial and construction success but cannot possibly do all the tasks alone. Only the facility manager should be in a position to delegate work. Facility managers might call this the Golden Rule: "The one with the gold, rules."

2. Despite the rules, construction managers, if not under the same area, may feel a need to run with the ball if given the chance. Facility managers must deal equitably in their management of all trades and disciplines. Never give an assignment that is beyond a person's skills. As an example, should a construction manager be responsible for selecting wall-covering patterns? Would you expect the furniture buyer to inspect the telecommunications installation?

3. The facility manager must follow up on all delegated assignments when they are due. The procedure outlined under meetings covers most delegated work. Additional assignments that occur between meetings are usually made verbally. The facility manager should note the work to be done and place it in the meeting's file for inclusion with the next meeting's new business.

4. If the assignment falls due prior to a meeting, follow up beforehand. Don't wait until the deadline is past. This is not a police action where you wait behind the billboard for someone to go through a stop sign so you can write a ticket. Emphasize the team effort—if an assignee fails, then the facility manager and the whole team fails. Remind the person of the upcoming deadline. No surprises from the people assigned to the tasks are necessary either. If they finish early, get the results early. If they cannot get the work done, encourage them to let the facility manager know as soon as possible.

Etiquette

During the peace meetings to settle the Vietnam war, several months were required to deal with a very sensitive area. The delegates had to decide on the size and shape of the meeting table. When that debate was finished, they debated where each person should sit.

Cause	Effect
Some facility managers feel that by sitting at the head of the table they command respect.	Tables are rectangular, and the longer the better.
Some facility managers feel that by sitting in the center of one side, they are more accessible. They downplay the leader and highlight the team effort.	These tables are not as long as the first example, or, if at all possible, they are round.
Some facility managers have meetings in the field—that is, at the site of the project—and they walk through the job.	A stand-up meeting sounds great because it may actually be shorter in length, and everyone can see firsthand what is happening. The negative aspect is that the team tends to wander.
Some facility managers have meetings in a field trailer on the site of a new construction.	The table is an old full height door, and the proceedings are a bit less formal. The door is a disguised rectangular table, so we have come full circle in our analysis.

Which method is the best? Which table should the furniture buyer purchase? They are all correct! The situation varies within each corporation for such reasons as:

- Personality of the facility manager
- Politics of the corporation
- Nature of the team members, especially the construction manager during the implementation phase
- Size and complexity of the project
- Location of the project in relation to the home base of the corporation, not the homes of the team members

Summary

Facility managers quite possibly will use different methods over time because the projects are different each time. A consistent approach makes for a known routine and makes the meetings move along.

- You are all professionals; do not waste time.
- Get to the point.
- Try to minimize side conversations.
- Try to keep the meeting in control by talking about one particular issue at a time.

- Do not let someone jump to another topic if it is completely unrelated to the issue being discussed.

- Zookeepers always feed the bears at the zoo, and you should feed the team at an early-morning meeting. Refreshments are a small price to pay for a well-run, well-attended project meeting.

- Make the facility manager's decisions if you are a facility manager. Don't avoid responsibility by asking for a show of hands.

Positive leaders get positive results. The team should know the whole project. No sense to separate the members so they are working in isolation. You *can* lead a team to the project and make them work.

3.5   The Words of Others—Project Management: An Approach

Ralph Mancini   *Chairman, Mancini-Duffy Associates*

The following are my comments on this chapter:

In Section 3.2, the responsibilities of the design firm and engineer are cited in a combined list. Most of those responsibilities listed are clearly those of the design firm. With reference to the fourth item under "Designer," the design firm coordinates with the engineer in relation to the design. Again, listed under the responsibilities of the engineer, the item concerning electrical delivery systems should be at the discretion of the designer.

In addition, in the table on p. 68, the "What" under "Business Plan" should read, in my opinion, "The overall business market and strategic plans must be defined." In the "What" of "Location Requirements," the words "and program" should be inserted after "business plans," to read "business plans *and program.*"

As to the "Technology" section of the table, I would like to note that sometimes the determination of telecommunications, etc., ties in with availability within the building. Telecommunications (as noted in another section of the table) should be planned and engineered before construction begins, so that it can be phased into the construction process.

Our views on managing the project meetings, Section 3.4, might be expressed as follows: The consultant on the project (space planner, interior designer, designer, architect, engineer, etc.) is the technical and creative "right arm" of the facilities manager. The consultant brings to meetings the latest technological advances available through his or her interaction with other consultants and clients.

At the inception of the project, the kickoff meeting will establish the scope of the project as it refers to:

- Space expansionSpace reduction
- Design criteria
- Function
- Furnishings (new or existing reused)
- Air-conditioning (normal or 24-hour)
- Intended budget
- Proposed move-in, etc.

In general, design firms must rely on the facility manager as the spokesperson for the corporation and as a liaison with management, and to set forth those guidelines necessary for the successful completion of the project.

It is the consultant's experience in interpreting the users' wants and the facilities management constraints that will make the project a success or a failure.

Second Stage: Applying the Basics to the Facility Management Process

4

Project Feasibility

4.1 Introduction

In 1949 or so, Parker Brothers introduced one of the first games devoted to project feasibility. This portion of a project requires the facility manager to answer some basic questions: Who? Where? How? You might recognize these three questions from the now-famous game Clue.

In the playing of *Clue,* a murder already has been committed, with a certain weapon in a certain room of Mr. Boddy's "palatial mansion." Through "the process of deduction and good plain common sense," the game player is expected to figure out the answer to the three questions.

During project feasibility, facility managers seek the answers to these same three questions, as follows:

Who

Facility managers are required to perform a program of the proposed relocating units. This is accomplished by your going from room to room as the player does in *Clue.* Asking the right questions will determine the *who* of the move. Instead of using the Detective Note Pad, you use programming forms.

In *Clue,* all the characters are fictitious; they include Col. Mustard, Miss Scarlet, Professor Plum, Mr. Green, Mrs. White, and Mrs. Peacock. Facility managers will not recognize most of the names uncovered during programming. Facility managers should be aware that the user's growth forecast possibly may fall in the same category as the six *Clue* characters: fiction!

The first section of this chapter, Programming, outlines the best process to follow to take the mystery out of the *who.*

Where

In *Clue,* the player has it made. The murder occurred in one of nine rooms: hall, lounge, dining room, kitchen, ballroom, conservatory, billiard room, library, or study. Facility managers managing a move to another city or even another building have a difficult time in pinpointing the correct solution. In the game, you know that the answer is neatly set aside in the little envelope sitting in the middle of the board. In real life, the facility manager must work with facts and figures to deduce the best single solution for the corporate move. Through proper financial forecasting, rational thinking, and accurate budgeting, management will be shown the solution which is the best move for the money.

The second section of this chapter outlines the necessary steps and procedures to show senior management the *where* for the corporate relocation.

How

In the game, the answer to "how" is one of six possible weapons: knife, candlestick, revolver, rope, lead pipe, wrench. In facilities management, "how" is the entire project process. The game player eliminates the weapons through deductive questioning; the facility manager uses another method. Why leave anything to chance? Produce a project schedule outlining all the various steps, events, and critical items that must occur in a timely manner.

The third section of this chapter delineates the essential points of "how."

To win at *Clue,* the player makes an accusation as to who murdered Mr. Boddy (one of the deadly six names), where it occurred (which room), and how the victim died (which weapon was used). The player looks in the solution envelope and, if correct, lays the three cards face up on the table and wins the game.

In corporate life, there may not be any winning. There certainly isn't a magic envelope with the final answers. If the project is not programmed properly, financially forecast accurately, or completed on schedule, then we already know:

- Who did the murder: facility manager
- Where: at the project site
- How: through facilities mismanagement
- The victim: the end user
- The accuser: senior management

Project feasibility contains the clues to avoid this scenario.

4.2   Programming

The purpose of a program is to gather any and all requirements to be used in the planning of space. The more accurate the response, the more accurate the floor plans will reflect the expected departmental growth and work flow.

No one correct format for gathering information exists. Use a form that easily captures essential information. The key elements of a program form follow.

- Title page (see Figure 4.1).
  - Project title.
  - Project location.
  - Facility manager.
  - User coordinator.
  - Name of individual interviewed.
  - Interview date.
  - Name of the person who prepared the program.

Division	Department				Chargeback code
Project title					
Building address	Floor	Zone	Current usable		Current rentable
Corporate facilities/project manager			Title		
Address	Floor	Zone	Telephone		
Departmental (user) coordinator			Title		
Address	Floor	Zone	Telephone		

Prepared by	Title	Date
Person interviewed	Title	Date
Reviewed and approved	Title	Date
Reviewed and approved	Title	Date

1. Provide the mission of your division or department including functional responsibilities.
2. Attach a current organizational chart of the department. Chart should reflect the department's relationship within corporation.
3. Provide a summary of significant operational changes under consideration during the life cycle of this forecast that would have an impact on your facilities.

Figure 4.1   Yourco facilities requirements and corporate personnel forecasts.

- Date prepared.
- Space for review and approval by the next level of senior management in the department.
- Space for review and approval by the next level of senior management, if appropriate.
- Date approved.
- Departmental summary.
  - Provide a brief written summary of the department's functional responsibilities.
  - Attach a current organizational chart that outlines the department and its relationship to the corporation.
- Planned changes.
  - Provide a brief summary of known operational changes in either staff or systems being considered during the planning cycle of this program. A planning cycle usually covers three time periods: existing or current staffing; time period one—let's say 2 years—the time of the expected completion of the project; time period two—let's say 5 years. Growth in larger corporations tends to get hazy after 6 months; therefore, 5 years is very rough and probably wrong.
- Adjacency (see Figure 4.2).
  - List any other departments which require contiguous adjacency and the reason for the adjacency. Surprisingly, adjacencies are frequently one-sided, with the other named department having a completely different adjacency need.
  - Further analyze adjacencies for prioritization into three classifications: mandatory, convenient, if possible.
  - Priority setting allows you the flexibility to stack departments according to needs.
- Conference requirements (see Figure 4.3).
  - List departmental conference needs by type of scheduled meetings held, frequency of the meeting, average duration of the meeting, average number of participants at the meeting.
  - This category applies to all meetings *held* not for the meetings *attended* by the individual.
  - In the case of two departments holding a joint meeting, reflect under one area and reference in the other.
  - Required special equipment should be included: audiovisual (screen, projectors), boards (marker, tack, chalk, chart rail), reading (bookshelves, magazine shelves), communications (speaker phone, teleconferencing).
- Auxiliary space (see Figure 4.3).
  - Capture special space needs separately. These special spaces are

4. Adjacency requirements Show departmental units that require contiguous adjacency to each other, provide code: (1) constant communication, (2) occasional, (3) little or none		
Unit name and letter	To unit	Nature of adjacency
A		
B		
C		
D		
E		
F		
G		
H		
I		
J		
K		
L		
M		

Identify if department as a whole or any significant division has a critical work-flow adjacency to another department within group; describe the nature of the requirement.

Figure 4.2 Yourco facilities requirements and corporate personnel forecasts; adjacency requirements.

usually the responsibility of the departmental manager and include reception rooms and lounges, conference rooms (not previously counted), staff service areas (kitchenette, vending machines), storage or file rooms, computer rooms, library, workrooms, testing rooms, laboratories, vaults (money, records, precious metals, artwork), warehouses, bathrooms (beyond building standard).

- Traffic (See Figure 4.4).
  - Provide for each unit within the department the typical number of people that visit the unit.
  - List internal visitors separately from external visitors. Use information for proximity to building entrance or elevators, reception

<table>
<tr><td colspan="11">5. Conference requirements
Indicate frequency and duration for average number of participants during
scheduled conferences initiated by your division on a weekly basis.
Equipment code: (1) visual, (2) chalk/tackboard, (3) telecommunications</td></tr>
</table>

Unit	1-6 staff	Dura-tion	6-12	Dura-tion	12-18	Dura-tion	Over 18	Dura-tion	Equip. Code	Comments
A										
B										
C										
D										
E										
F										
G										
H										
I										
J										
K										
L										
M										

<table>
<tr><td>6. Auxiliary space requirements
Indicate special space needs, such as file room, storage room, library, work
room, testing room, etc.; if existing, indicate approximate usable sq ft.</td></tr>
</table>

1.	sq ft
2.	sq ft
3.	sq ft
4.	sq ft
5.	sq ft

Figure 4.3 Yourco facilities requirements and corporate personnel forecasts; conference requirements.

room needs (including size and seating capacity), and coat room sizing.

- General files (see Figure 4.4).
  - Account for individual filing needs within the workstation.
  - Calculate general departmental files. File needs are not measured in number of drawers in a file cabinet but rather in total linear inches of filing capacity used in existing time period. Forecast for future filing needs in the other two time periods. Files stored in conventional letter and lateral files can be quickly combined for total needs.

Unit	Typical day		Peak day		Comments on nature and duration
	Internal	Public	Internal	Public	
A					
B					
C					
D					
E					
F					
G					
H					
I					
J					
K					
L					
M					

7. Internal and external visitor traffic
Indicate for typical day the number of people from outside your department
who visit. Separate internal and public visitors.

8. Departmental filing requirements Indicate total linear inches of filing material required.	Time periods		
	1	2	3
1. Legal-size material			
2. Letter-size material			
3. Indicate other size file material:			
4.			
5.			
6.			

Figure 4.4 Yourco facilities requirements and corporate personnel forecasts;
internal and external visitor traffic.

- Individual requirements (see Figure 4.5).
  - List every existing position within each department with columns for each of the three time periods (existing, time periods one and two).
  - Include square footage per level and a column for the extension of number of people multiplied by square feet for each of the three periods.
- Summary.
  - Convert all the various departmental needs into square feet. The sum is "net usable square feet." This excludes the space needed for access to each workstation. This missing space is the *circulation factor,* which is a percentage applied to the net usable square feet.

				Personnel			Special service			Std.	Usable sq ft		

9. Detailed requirements
Indicate each function by department, list internal adjacency, show number of
staff per function for three time periods, indicate any special services required.
standard allocation and usable square feet to be completed by facilities mgmt.

Division									Department				Chargeback code

#	Function	Adj. no.	Personnel			Special service			Std. all	Usable sq ft		
			1	2	3	Elec.	Tele.	Other		1	2	3
1												
2												
3												
4												

Remarks, comments	Subtotal usable sq ft			
	Circulation factor @ ___ %			
	Total usable sq ft			
	Total rentable sq ft			

Figure 4.5 Yourco facilities requirements and corporate personnel forecasts; detailed requirements.

- Use a factor of 25 to 30 percent in closed planning.
- Use a factor of 25 to 35 percent in open planning. The range varies because of the following criteria: proximity of one workstation to another, type of space (customer contact through operations), layout and design.

Accuracy

The final program contains highly confidential information outlining current staffing, future growth projections, hiring plans, marketing ideas, and other corporate strategy. Yet the information gathered is from department managers who should know their own needs and fully understand work flow requirements.

However, the overall corporate long-range plans may not be part of the manager's knowledge. Additionally, the overall division head may have plans for reorganization or other changes that are not contained within any one department. The division head may not agree with departmental forecasts for personnel changes (increases or decreases).

Completed programs should be approved by the division head or the senior manager of the area. Similar reasoning leads the facility manager to seek higher approval when more than one division has been programmed.

The current or existing column of requirements can be used for any churn work prior to the move. Use this information to determine the functionality of the space, to see how tight or loose the conditions are within the department, and as a check for conformance with local codes. The interim period forecast may be required by the facility manager if the move will occur after this period's date.

The program information for small moves or churn projects can be done at a single interview. For a major relocation involving a significant number of staff, the techniques may be altered.

I recommend forwarding the questionnaire directly to the interviewee in advance. The manager can complete as much information as possible prior to the interview. This allows the programmer to minimize interview time.

Programming process

The programming process is based on an external consultant firm's being employed by the facility manager.

- Provide consultant with the following information:
  - Number of interviews, name and telephone number of each interviewee.
  - Two future time periods (in addition to current).
  - Approximate number of employees to be moved.
  - Special analysis required.
  - Current organizational chart indicating the affected department(s).
- Have consultant prepare questionnaire.
- Send a memorandum, with a sample questionnaire, to each manager to be interviewed, outlining:

- Purpose of the program.
- Programming process.
- Who will be conducting the program.
- What each manager will be required to supply.
- What to expect from the program.
- What to do with the completed questionnaires (to whom they should be returned).

- Prepare questionnaires for distribution, type in name of department and manager, and supply other pertinent information.

- Distribute questionnaires:
  - At a general meeting attended by managers responsible for completing forms. These groups should be limited to 15 to 20 managers at a time.
  - Via corporate interoffice mail, the fastest way to distribute the forms.

- Have managers complete forms and return to you. Retain a copy and send to consultant.

- Have consultant analyze forms for completeness and any potential problem areas.

- Arrange for consultant to interview each manager, with the following goals in mind:
  - Complete any missing information.
  - Resolve any problem areas or concerns.
  - Walk through the department to review its operation.
  - Create a personal working relationship with the manager.

- Have consultant analyze final results after in-person interviews. Most consultant firms utilize computer programs that can convert the data quickly into many versions for review.

- Review the program analysis. Any changes are made at this point.

- Have consultant revise data and present a final report with recommendations on:
  - Quantity of square footage required.
  - Quantity of new furniture required.
  - Growth rate forecast.
  - Adjacency and stacking of departments.

- Have managers review and approve the program results.

- Use approved program information as basis for the interior design process.

The finished program is the first essential piece of the project feasibility phase. The second criterion is the financial budgeting and forecasting, which follows in the next section.

4.3 Facility Financial Forecasting and Budgeting

Forecasting is something that should never have been allowed. It should never have been started, and its continuation is the ruination of all people, including facility managers.

Forecasting the outcome of any sports event has led to widespread betting. Every newspaper reports the odds of winning or losing. As soon as a facility manager makes a forecast, there will be odds on its happening on time or within budget.

Forecasting the weather has led meteorologists to have humorous attitudes (since they seldom seem to be right). Do we remember a correct forecast? No, we remember the forecast for sunny weather when it rains. Meteorologists have adopted the *partly* forecast, "Today's weather will be partly cloudy." This proves to be a safer bet.

Facility forecasting involves the timeliness of a massive amount of events that occur between 3 and 36 months from the time of your forecast. Unsuccessful forecasts lead to apologies, explanations, and future unemployment! Obviously, the solution to forecasting is to wait until the sports event, the day's weather pattern, or the project is completed. You can be 100 percent correct every time.

Unfortunately, senior management would like to know the results *now*. Therefore, you might as well be the best you can be. The facility financial forecast is derived from senior management's uncertainty of timing and costs, and their desire to have these facts in advance.

Your future employment is wagered on an estimated cost which will be subjected to events you cannot possibly anticipate. As with the "partly cloudy" forecast, hedge your position and your estimate with positive steps to ensure the best forecast.

The World Book Dictionary definition of forecasting is: "the act or process of predicting on the basis of present trends, of probable conditions or events to come...." This section covers:

- Criteria to be included in the forecast
- Categories of expenditures
- Exploring alternatives/you get what you pay for
- Timing the forecast
- How to report the real numbers to management

Criteria to be included in the forecast

Some facility managers feel that getting "good numbers" is the most important criterion for a forecast. Some facility managers feel that getting a schedule of events first is the most important criterion. These feelings are both wrong!!! The most important aspect of a financial forecast is the *project rationale*.

What does senior management look for first? Proof that the proposed investment conforms with overall business strategy and management plans.

The project rationale gives you:

- Opportunity to justify the proposed expenditures
- Factors that went into the business decision
- Complete description of the project
- List of major issues and risks associated with the project

Although it would take far too long to list everything that could be included in the rationale, listed below are 16 essential items.

1. Provide a statement of the purpose and need for the project. This should be simple, straightforward, and strictly based on business needs.
2. Describe the type of facility, its capacity, and its purpose. Types can include major buildings, branches, warehouses, etc.
3. Make an assessment of the project's impact on current facilities, and how this project will integrate with present facilities.
4. Review the future projects that may develop as a result of this project, including outstanding lease obligations or churn expense to backfill an area that will be vacated as a result of the project.
5. Reconcile these costs with the capital expenditure plans. You as facility manager will be wise to remember that with any bit of success this forecast will come back to haunt you in 2 or 3 years.
6. Examine personnel issues, including demographics, availability of new hires, impact on current staffing, and cost to relocate staff that is moving to new site.
7. Timing is important. There should be timetables, milestones, key dates, and costs associated with each major completion. Always include time to have your forecast approved and your rationale circulated to all required corporate levels. Timetables are the project's backbone. As an example, on a major building project you must account for such time-consuming items as identifying a property, planning, designing, and engineering before you get to construction. Construction is the longest phase, and you might break it down into three substeps for each major trade:

    a. Bidding/awarding

    b. Approvals/fabrication

    c. General construction

These three phases would then have specific start and finish dates for such major trades as:

    a. Excavation and foundation

    b. Structural steel

    c. Concrete

    d. Curtainwall

    e. Drywall

    f. Elevators and escalators

    g. Heating, ventilation, and air conditioning (HVAC)

    h. Plumbing

    i. Fire protection

    j. Electrical

8. Consider the project's relationship to your corporate and divisional macro/long-range plans and objectives. (Informing senior management that a business is relocating to another state 30 days prior to the move is a major error!)

9. Indicate leased space requirements, incremental space, and costs shown in cost per square foot, length of corporate commitment, cancellation clause, associated costs to cancel, renewal provisions and costs, and any unusual terms, such as requiring you to remove a specific installation (i.e., kitchens, raised flooring) at lease termination.

10. In new building situations, an environmental audit for toxicity and other harmful substances must be performed. "New" means not previously occupied by your corporation. Other important criteria in this category are:

    a. Building appraisals

    b. Building conditions report for older facilities

    c. Insurability of the facility

11. Establish conformance with local, state, and federal fire, safety, and health standards. When applicable, set up conformance with your own corporate guidelines and standards.

12. Special problems handling requires analysis of:

    a. Transportation for staff access to the site

    b. Mail delivery

    c. Garbage removal

    d. Utilities availability

    e. Telecommunications hookups

    f. Other distribution and operational considerations

13. Investigate risks associated with the project. The three major issues that occur are:

    a. Economic and business market conditions

    b. Contingencies and constraints

    c. Legal and regulatory situations

These first 13 items should provide enough information to get you to the "partly cloudy" forecast! Now, you can concentrate on the numbers.

14. Estimate the cost of the project and any subsequent investment that will result from this project. An example of a subsequent investment might be:

    a. Cost to purchase land and to erect an office building on the property

    b. Cost to build out the interior space for the proposed corporate department

    c. Cost to furnish the department with new furniture and equipment

    d. Cost to physically relocate the unit

    e. Cost to renovate the space vacated by the unit for the next occupant

    f. Cost to buy out the lease

    g. Cost to write off any undepreciated assets

15. Compose a statement of major assumptions used to derive the incremental income forecasts that result from project's completion.

16. Projects that don't achieve corporate goals require that sufficient reasons and financial justification be provided to justify the project to management.

The Project Rationale is a long document filled with schedules and details well beyond a senior executive's available time. The detail will be read and thoroughly analyzed by other staff members.

I suggest you write a summary cover memorandum. This memo should be short, one or two pages in length, and should summarize all 16 items. Suggested paragraph titles for the cover memorandum are:

- Purpose

- Project description, including cost and size

- Financial summary, highlighting benefits and net impact

- Rationale

Categories of expenditures

When compiling the various anticipated expenditures, consider all aspects of the project. To ensure that no costs are missed, I recommend you follow the flow of the project to capture all costs.

The following are major expenses incurred during the project life cycle.

- Real estate selection phase
  - Brokerage fees
  - Architectural fees
  - Environmental studies, toxicity reports, traffic studies, demographic reports
  - Market research reports for business markets
  - Test borings on site
  - Lawyer's fees
  - Relocation firms to search areas, staff housing
  - Insurance
  - Financing expenses

- Feasibility study phase
  - Architectural fees
  - Interior design fees
  - Engineering fees, including, among others, mechanical and electrical; plumbing, structural, and acoustical; civil engineering and landscape architects

- Design development phase
  - More architectural, design, and engineering fees
  - Kitchen and cafeteria consultants, as required
  - Rendering fees and other specialists

- Contract document phase
  - Still more consultant fees for all disciplines
  - Estimator's fees
  - Telecommunications fees

- Purchasing phase
  - Cost to purchase, lease, or rent furniture, carpeting, accessories, signage, window treatments
  - Cost to purchase artwork, sculptures
  - Cost to landscape, plant, and pave parking areas
  - Telecommunications equipment purchase, delivery, and installation
  - Construction items
  - All applicable local, state, and federal sales and use taxes

- Construction phase
  - Site demolition, site utilities, site work, landscaping, and paving
  - Excavation, concrete foundation, vault construction, concrete superstructure, masonry, and stonework

- Structural steel, metal deck, miscellaneous iron, and ornamental metal
- Roofing, waterproofing, flashing, and caulking
- Hollow metal, roll-up truck dock doors, windows, mirrors, and miscellaneous glass
- Hardware, acoustic tile, rough carpentry and drywall, and spray fireproofing
- Ceramic and mosaic tile, resilient flooring, louvers, painting, lobby work
- Toilet partitions, toilet accessories
- Window-washing rig, elevators and escalators
- All heating, ventilation, and air-conditioning work
- Plumbing—sprinklers and electrical

- Occupancy phase
  - Moving and relocation expenses
  - Severance pay
  - Temporary personnel expenses
  - Training expenses for new employees
  - Advertising for new employees
  - Computer and other technical equipment relocation costs, including dismantling, shipping, and reassembly
  - Postal, stationery, and related expenses

- Postoccupancy phase
  - Warranty and maintenance expenses beyond the warranty period
  - Sale of old furniture
  - Write-off of undepreciated assets at old site
  - Cost either to renovate space or to market former space
  - Postoccupancy evaluation to determine staff acceptance of the change

- Contingencies for the unexpected
  - Do not omit a contingency factor. There is always the chance that you did leave something out, or the unanticipated will occur.
  - Rule of thumb—if your corporation does not have guidelines or limitations—is 10 percent on top of all variable expenses. A known cost, such as a lease rental rate fixed for 10 years, does not require a contingency.
  - The percentage method is preferred over the "round every number up" method. This way you can rely on estimates based on logic.

While this list may not be all-inclusive, it is sufficient to keep you busy. Very few of us can do all these estimates without other professional assistance. This assistance comes from other qualified individuals on your staff, within your corporation, or from external professional consultant firms.

Exploring alternatives: You get what you pay for

The truth in your numbers becomes important later in the project. Obviously, the more attention you pay up front, the less awesome your task and the less time required later trying to reconcile a bad estimate to a real cost.

Alternative methods to facility financial forecasting are available. Cost per square foot is the most utilized method.

A senior manager is likely to ask, "If we were to build a new building, what would it cost?" You could ask for 6 months to analyze the request, or answer, "That would be $175 per square foot, not counting land." Or, the request may be for installing 35,000 square feet of carpet tile. You respond, "It will cost $3 per square foot, installed." (Facility managers seldom talk in square yards!)

Nothing wrong with these guesses. They may actually be right. This kind of estimate leaves room for working out the level of finishes and details. On the other hand, as additional items get added to the project, senior management has a habit of remembering only that initial cost-per-square-foot figure.

It is best to have your estimate and the associated assumptions to fall back on when the eventual change of scope occurs. Another alternative is receiving your estimates in a bracket of ranges (see Table 4.1). Given the figures in Table 4.1, do you go with a conservative, low-end estimate of $4,700,000? Do you go for broke and use the high end of $6,550,000? Do you straddle the fence and take a mean of $5,625,000? Let's examine each alternative to see the recommended solution:

- Go with the low end of the range to make yourself look like a winner. While this may get quick management approval, you may find that you cannot pay for what was specified during the project's contract document phase. I recommend not to go with the low numbers

TABLE 4.1   Yourco, Inc., Project Cost Estimates

Item	Low estimate	Mean estimate	High estimate
Consultant fees	$ 500,000	$ 575,000	$ 650,000
Furniture/furnishings	$1,200,000	$1,550,000	$1,900,000
Construction	$3,000,000	$3,500,000	$4,000,000
Total estimates:	$4,700,000	$5,625,000	$6,550,000

unless you are prepared to buy the low end of construction and furniture items.

■ Go with the high end of the range to protect yourself. This alternative affords you more than enough funding. This is particularly true when you add on a contingency factor of 10 percent. The problem is that too many high numbers leads to the world's most expensive facilities project and to senior management's rejection of the cost proposal. The conclusion of a project that utilized high numbers willshow a "save." This sounds attractive, but this approach is quickly seen through by management. Subsequent requests for funding will be subject to more detailed management analysis.

■ Utilize the mean or average of the ranges. You may also rest easier if your corporation allows contingencies. The facility manager can cover most of the higher range with this extra funding. The problem with this method is that the average is never the right number. Your estimate is not tied into anything. As an example, if the furniture estimate range was based on plastic laminate finishes for the low number and wood finishes for the high, then what is the mean? You might argue for wood in private offices and plastic laminate elsewhere. However, in a typical project the mean number does not make too much sense.

I recommend *all of the above* with a bit of professional opinion weighing the three alternatives. The answer entails your analyzing each component of the line items to determine the best estimate. Therefore, you might select the *high* fees, the *low* furniture estimate, and the *high* construction estimate. At least this way your numbers can be backed with a logical approach and a rational explanation.

Timing the forecast

Long-range forecasting occurs if your corporation has a long-range space plan tied into a capital expenditure plan. The most critical thing to remember during the future time frames of your forecast is inflation. Items will tend to cost more in the future.

Some rules of thumb include 7 percent increase per annum in construction costs and 5 percent for furniture items. It is normal to feel somewhat insecure and at great risk with these long-range forecasts.

Fortunately, the larger the corporation, the greater the chances that the project will be:

■ Canceled outright

■ Reorganized because of business reasons

- Changed because of a new manager in charge of the unit
- Assigned to someone else

Normally, a project should be estimated as part of the annual business planning cycle. If your corporation is on a calendar-year basis, January to December, then the early fall is your timing. Estimates should be worked on during the third quarter and submitted to line management for inclusion with their business plans.

Do not expect to start a project in January on the basis of third- or fourth-quarter approvals. It is almost impossible to get long-lead construction or furniture items on such short notification.

Plan ahead. The worst timing is the eleventh hour when the "computer is on the truck dock" or "the furniture arrived; when will the construction be completed?" Forecasts should definitely be part of the normal business cycle. It is incumbent on facilities managers to ensure that business managers do not submit a plan without the facilities portion.

Equity allocation process.   Approval of the business/facility plan is not necessarily a green light to spend the funds. As an example, it may represent the approval of the concept or overall financial package for the business. Corporations may require a detailed financial requisition or major expenditure proposal at the time the project actually gets under way.

The three-part process of forecasting and monetary request is called an equity allocation and capital expenditure process.

The first step of the equity allocation process focuses on certain major projects that will result in long-term commitments or that are strategic in nature. Undertaking of these projects will result in a directional change in business.

The second step is the major expenditure proposal. As outlined elsewhere in this chapter, this provides the specific details regarding the business rationale and financial impact of the project. This is done just at the time the funds will be required. This ensures up-to-date financial information, current business planning, and the best forecast of timing to complete the project.

The third step, and perhaps the most ignored, is the follow-up. The follow-up involves procedures to monitor the performance of the project against forecasts projected in the major expenditure proposal. This is not a variation of regular status and financial update reports during the life cycle of a project. This process requires filing of status reports when the project is completed. This first report is the final status of the project. Thereafter, the reports should be done annually for up to 3 years.

How do you report the real numbers to senior management?

Each corporation has detailed procedures for reporting financial information. However, the circumstances of discovering that the project is running over the forecast creates the dilemma of reporting the *real* numbers to senior management.

It is always amazing that the same senior manager who signed your expenditure proposal, and sought your assurance not to exceed the amount, will be the cause of your problems. It is this same manager who continually makes changes during the project (and the facility manager tends to accommodate these changes). The results of one change too many is called an overrun.

An overrun is particularly difficult for a facility manager because it means that you have exhausted all available funds, including any contingency amount. Furthermore, it casts doubt on your forecasting abilities, your managerial skills in completing a project on budget, and your original rationale.

If you had difficulty writing the rationale, try writing the explanation for the overrun. Basically, within normal forecasting and contingency allowance, a presentation of an overrun rationale and request would mean that the project is at least 20 percent over the original forecast.

I recommend a very straightforward solution. Tell the truth. In most cases, the facility manager needs to go over the same rationale and assumptions to reconcile why extra funds should be appropriated to the project.

Some corporations take a hard line on overruns—including a stipulation that absolutely no extra funds can even be committed by a facility manager without receiving the written approval of senior management.

The real message from management is that the facility manager is going to be held accountable, and you better be constantly monitoring the project.

The nature of forecasting.   A final note on forecasting: A college president in New Jersey made a startling financial statement that keeps forecasting in perspective. The college president said, "The cost of education in the university has *not* increased in the last 30 years, nor will it increase in the next 20 years. In 1957, the cost of one year's tuition at the university was equal to the price of a new Chevrolet. And today, in 1987, the cost of one year's tuition is still equal to the price of a new Chevrolet. Furthermore, it would still probably be equal to the price of a new Chevrolet in 2007!"

Unfortunately, most facility managers cannot relate their forecasts in this manner; otherwise, we would be dealing in fleet management!

It is obvious—financial budgeting and forecasting is a significant facility management responsibility. Usually facility managers have at least one person on staff who is an expert at number crunching. After all, the backbone of the project is the rationale, along with the proper financial analysis.

Operating and maintenance budget accounts

In addition to the various facility capital expenditures outlined, it is equally important to include forecasts and budgets for day-to-day operating and maintenance expenses. There are several types of forecast techniques utilized in a corporation. The more popular methods are:

- Life cycle costing
- Zero-based budgeting
- Standard budgeting (current cost plus escalations)

Life cycle costing. The facility manager calculates normal or periodic expenses for each budget line item. This enables the forecast to indicate the year when additional funding will be required for maintenance and repairs.

Examples of expenditures that are not necessarily repeated year after year or month to month, if a 1-year budget is being done, include:

- Painting of office space
- Snow removal
- Lawn and landscaping
- Mechanical equipment replacement
- Reroofing/waterproofing
- Insect/rodent control
- Building exterior repairs

Zero-based budgeting. The facility manager must justify each and every expenditure, each year. In other words, the corporation assumes that no funds are required for any line item unless it is substantiated as a necessary cost.

This method is advantageous for the corporation since one-time expenses and other unusual expenses do not repeat as "extra" available funds to be spent by the facility manager. Phantom funds drop out because they cannot be rationalized.

This method can be dangerous if unexpected funds are required. The facility manager must go back to senior management for the extra funds. There is generally more work on the facility manager's part under this method.

Standard budgeting.   This is the most used method in which known costs from one year become the basis for forecasting the next year's (or years') expenses. This is fairly simple for facility managers. The only forecasting required is to predict the escalation in expenses over the next year.

Some increases are known at the outset of the budget cycle. For example, the announcement of an increase in electric or telephone rates is usually released well in advance of its occurrence. Maintenance expenses for equipment are usually billed on an even amount each month and are known for the upcoming 12 months.

Budget line items

There are many levels of expenses that can be included within a facility manager's responsibilities. Budget expenses are listed below that are required for operating buildings. Some items listed under maintenance and repairs also require preventive maintenance expenditures.

In some cases, there are opportunities to generate income. These should be carried as "negative" expenses to offset real expenses.

- Rental expenses
  - Land costs
  - Lease expenses
  - Sublease income
  - Escalations
  - Insurance
  - Miscellaneous

- Utilities
  - Electric
  - Heating (electric, gas, oil)
  - Water
  - Energy savings or solar energy credits
  - Sewer
  - Miscellaneous

- Maintenance and repairs
  - Grounds: landscaping, pavements, parking, snow removal
  - Roofs
  - Exterior building repairs
  - Interior repairs, painting
  - Heating, ventilation and air-conditioning systems

- Mechanical, plumbing, electrical systems
- Life safety
- Security
- Kitchen equipment, cafeteria, food services
- Telecommunications
- Technology
- Elevators, escalators, conveyors
- Signage
- Miscellaneous

- Custodial
  - Rubbish/trash removal
  - Window repair, cleaning
  - Insect/rodent control
  - Janitorial
  - Carpet maintenance (shampooing, patching)
  - Window treatments (shades, blinds, drapes)
  - Uniforms and clothing
  - Automotive (fuel, oil, maintenance)
  - Miscellaneous

- Personnel
  - Salaries (straight time, overtime)
  - Temporary expenses
  - Consultant or contract employees
  - Benefits (sick leave, vacation, insurance, union, retirement)
  - Special events
  - Miscellaneous

Summary

When you're looking for *the* financial wizard, keep in mind the following interview technique:

A facility manager was once looking to hire a new financial analyst, someone who was on the "wizard with numbers" level. The local recruitment agency ("headhunter") had prequalified four candidates. The first candidate's credentials were presented and they were entirely satisfactory.

The facility manager explained for the next 30 minutes about the "ins and outs" of facility financial forecasting and budgeting (as outlined in this chapter).

The applicant was very excited about the position.

The facility manager asked, "Would you mind taking a simple, little test?"

"No, not at all" was the reply.

The facility manager asked, "How much is *one* plus *one*?"

"Why that's easy: *two*."

The facility manager said, "I'll get back to you."

The next applicant listened to the same outline of facility financial forecasting and agreed to the test.

The answer to the same test: *two*.

The third applicant also responded, "Two."

The fourth candidate came in, listened, and agreed to the test.

The facility manager asked, "How much is *one* plus *one?*"

The applicant said, "How much would you like it to be?"

The financial wizard was hired *immediately!*

4.4 Scheduling

In the best Scots dialect I could find, the poet Burns gave us: "The best laid schemes o' mice an' men, Gang aft agley, And lea'e us nought but grief and pain, For promised joy."

The World Book Dictionary defines schedule as "a written or printed statement of details; the time fixed for the doing of something." A few listings down is that of scheme, "a program of action; plan...a system of connected things, parts, or thoughts."

The facility manager, as outlined in the budgeting section, has completed the project rationale. One of the critical items to be included is the schedule or scheme that will be followed for the completion of the project. The schedule is a list of project items and events that must occur by certain dates to achieve its successful completion.

This section examines various methods of scheduling. Schedules are certainly easily computerized. However, the intent is to explain the methodology and thinking behind the schedule. This section also highlights the "grief and pain" of the facility team coping with the schedule.

A schedule is virtually useless if, once produced and published, it is not updated and followed up by the facility manager. All team members should be disciplined to adhere to their appointed dates. A schedule is a concise way to list all responsibilities and due dates in a neat package.

PERT

PERT stands for Program Evaluation Review Technique. A buzzword acronym that originated from the initials of a computerized management system that was developed for the handling of complex programs. The production of a missile or a spaceship is an example of where a PERT program would be used.

A massive computerized network of interrelated events may be helpful on a large building complex or similar project. The facility manager's need for this degree of control is usually overkill. On churn projects, the facility manager would spend more time maintaining the PERT than is actually spent on the renovation.

Critical path

Most consultant firms produce schedules manually. Consultants can update schedules right at the project meeting. The marked-up changes are brought back to the consultant's office for final updating. The changes are drafted, blueprinted, and distributed to all involved parties.

The schedules on the larger projects reflect the various lists of events or items on the left-hand column and the length of the project (time) across the top of the schedule. Each item is plotted for expected start and completion date.

Obviously, common sense and logic must prevail in completing the schedule. It is difficult to dig a foundation if the property is not identified; or erect a wall if the plasterboard is not ordered. (Although strange things *do* happen on projects.)

When all the events are listed in logical, chronological order, the facility manager has a sense of scope and timing for all planned events. If the chart is analyzed properly, a singular line of events emerges that is known as the critical path. These are items and events that, above all, must absolutely occur to keep the project moving on time. Certain events may slip without impact on the final completion date. Any change in dates for items on the critical path will definitely change the project schedule. The critical path allows you to pay extra attention to those events that are essential to the project's success.

One occasionally overlooked event—essential to the critical path of the schedule—is time for senior management's approval of the project's financing. Project rationales must be listed in the schedule. With any delays in funding approval, a project usually misses the completion date. At first, delays in approval are sometimes not apparent. Long-lead items, such as hardware, may not be delivered on time later in the project owing to early money approval delays.

A sample schedule of events for a churn project is reflected in Table 4.2.

Seat-of-the-pants/dress

Any facility manager who attempts to do scheduling from pure guesswork is asking for big problems. This seat-of-the-pants/dress, shoot-

TABLE 4.2   Yourco, Inc., Sample Project Schedule

Event	Project weeks															
	1	2	3	4	5	6	7	8	9	10	11	12	13	14	15	16
1. Design development	X	X	X													
2. Design approval	X	X														
3. Preliminary budget	X	X	X	X												
4. Contract Documents		X	X	X	X	X	X									
5. Bidding				X	X	X	X									
6. Final $$$ approvals						X	X	X								
7. Furniture procurement								X	X	X	X	X	X	X	X	X
8. Construction								X	X	X	X	X	X	X	X	
9. Furniture installation												X	X	X		
10. Telecommunications									X	X	X	X	X	X	X	X
11. Move-in															X	X
12. Complete punchlist														X	X	X
13. Close-out project															X	X

from-the-hip method is the one most encouraged within a corporation. A facility manager conducts more scheduling meetings in the elevators than in the office. The scenario is repeated every day:

The facility manager gets on the elevator fresh from a job meeting on a project on the twentieth floor. On the way down, a senior manager from the fourteenth floor gets on the elevator. The manager inquires, "When will the project for fourteen be completed?" The facility manager should respond, "I don't know at this time, but I'll get back to you shortly with the timing." Instead, the facility manager replies, "By the end of May." Unfortunately, the manager will remember this date. The facility manager is advised not to guess out loud. Not knowing the exact date of each event of each project is okay within the corporate life. You'll be remembered for the bad guess. Always be sure to get back with the date.

Corporate mandated move date

It is always amazing that there is never enough time to do something right the first time, but there is enough time to do it over again if it is not correct. Senior management will try to force specific dates for moves or project completions.

These dates usually have sound thinking supporting them—for example, the advertised opening of a new branch, the commencement of a new service with a hot line telephone service, the relocation of a business, the purchasing of another company with signage to be changed, or a date by which the reorganization will be in effect.

If the facility manager was brought in at the conception of the change, rather than in the middle of the process, the chances of completing the project on schedule would be greatly increased.

Schedule complaints

It is interesting to see the progression of complaints about scheduling or a schedule as the project progresses. A typical scenario might go like this:

- Business managers complain to senior management about the date management selected to commence a new business. "There isn't enough time to hire and train the proper staff."

- Facility managers complain to the business manager that there isn't enough time to get the plans designed and bid. The furniture needs to be ordered before the plans will be done, "I need a bid exception. I need overtime money for *this one*."

- Real estate brokers complain to the facility manager that there isn't enough time to analyze the market for this business. "You just cannot pick any location."

- Designers complain to the facility manager that there isn't enough time on this job to be creative. After all, the new business needs the right atmosphere.

- Designers complain to the brokers that the found space is not workable for this function.

- Engineers complain to the facility manager that the schedule doesn't allow for the proper wiring of the space.

- Engineers complain to designers about the designer's lack of sensitivity for engineering concerns.

- Contractors complain to the facility manager that all the time for the project has been taken up with designing and engineering. The facility manager left insufficient time for the contractor to build the job. "I'll need overtime; I'll need to buy out items; I'll need three extra weeks."

- Contractors complain to designers that the layout specifies hard-to-get items.

- Telecommunication managers complain that there isn't enough room for the switch. "We'll be working all weekend because of this schedule just to get minimal service in for this business."

- Furniture buyers complain to the facility manager that "eight weeks are required for this type of furniture and you didn't allow for installation."

- Furniture buyers complain to designers that their specifications were not complete.

- Furniture buyers complain to the contractor that "your workers are standing on my new furniture."

- Movers complain to the facility manager that "I can't work with the other trades still in the way."

- Business managers complain to the facility manager, "I didn't think you'd make the date. Can't you move the date back a week?"

Yet, somehow (thanks to facility *teamwork*), the project gets completed on time, close to budget, and the business commences.

What would a schedule be like if someone didn't complain along its route? No one likes to work under the pressure of a schedule (even when the schedule is *exactly* what that discipline requested).

All parties are represented at the project meetings where the schedule is reviewed. It is not a good idea to update a schedule for a discipline not present at the meeting. They deny the ability to meet the changed date with "You should have waited until I got there."

Regardless of method used, it is a good idea to computerize the schedules. There are just too many projects and events for you to track. Although facility managers tend to have good memories, don't chance missing that one event.

A computerized list should include a linked dependency of events. That is, if one event in the link of events is changed, then all dependent events in the sequence should reflect date changes.

Some schedules show the range of dates within which each event may occur. This would show up on the schedule as "early start, late start, early finish, late finish." When there is no difference in a date, the same date would appear in the early and late slot. This technique allows the team to see all pertinent time parameters.

Summary

The old rule of thumb states that "80 percent of the work gets done in 20 percent of the time." Scheduling prompts new versions of this rule.

- Senior management.
  - 100 percent of the work *will* be done in 65 percent of the time, and under budget.
- Business manager.
  - 110 percent of the work will be done in 90 percent of the time. (*110 percent?*)
- Designer.

- 20 percent of the work should be done in 80 percent of the time—i.e., design work.
- Engineer.
  - 99.5 percent of the work will be done in 99.5 percent of the time.
- Construction manager.
  - 100 percent of the work will be done in 110 percent of the time—50 percent in overtime.
- Facility manager.
  - 0 percent of the work will be done unless I get financial approval. Then: 100 percent of the work will be done with 0 percent variation from the schedule.

4.5 The Words of Others—Project Feasibility

Ronald J. Goodrich *Senior Programmer, Interior Facilities Associates, Inc.*

Another type of programming and feasibility analysis, associated more with macro- and microplanning time frames, is available to the facility manager. This strategic planning for facilities utilization, or strategic programming, examines the big picture—linking future space needs to the business plan and developing appropriate real estate strategies to respond to emerging business conditions.

How much space is likely to be needed in future time periods? What kinds of space? Where will this space be located? Should it be leased or built? With a developer or without? How will a building project that might emerge from this planning be financed? This type of planning may lead to a specific project and a feasibility analysis—e.g., building a new headquarters complex. Or it may lead to a long-term facilities strategy that links space needs over time to emerging business conditions.

This strategic planning process precedes a specific project feasibility analysis. It is an overview rather than a justification of a single design project. It provides senior management with a review of alternatives, a justification for the selection of one over the others, and the costs associated with each.

The programming for this type of feasibility analysis differs somewhat from the more project-oriented program that the author describes. It is a "what-if" analysis, an examination of options before a specific project is selected and justified. While the methodology is the same, the information and analysis is different.

In a series of interviews, typically with senior management, the programmer gathers information on three topics—business drivers, personnel growth related to business growth, and business trends. Business drivers include an examination of new products, markets, technologies, or services that might be offered; political and organizational changes; acquisitions; and industry trends. Personnel projections are related to these business conditions, and emerging trends give conservative, optimistic, and likely scenarios of space need.

The finished program provides an overall picture of future space requirements. It establishes a range of requirements, with a low, likely, and high estimate for different growth projections. It identifies major units, their range of requirements, and the kinds of space needed. The range of space required is matched against space availability in each planning period. Strategies for dealing with each of the major contingencies are delineated.

This analysis graphically describes to management future space needs; these are linked to the growth and change in the business. With this information and overview, management can begin real estate planning. How much space? What kinds of space? Where? When will it be needed? With this long-term perspective, the facility manager can explore alternatives and develop more short-term or intermediate plans.

Project specific planning, as the author so aptly describes the process, is directed to justifying and designing a particular project. A danger, because everyone involved wants the project to "go," is to skew the feasibility analysis with unrealistic assumptions—build a case for the desired outcome. A facility manager, as a space planner and professional, needs to remain slightly skeptical. The facility manager should be able to step back and ask, "Does this project make sense?" A good manager is an able advocate for a project he or she believes in but maintains an organizational perspective.

The programming consultant and the facility manager should consider *alternatives* in doing a feasibility analysis. These alternatives may not even be presented; they may be fallback positions or options to consider in further planning. The level of quality for the finishes or furniture may be reduced to save money. Scheduling changes might be examined to respond to deadline concerns. Management looks to the facility manager to propose alternatives, as well as technical solutions, so that the business objective can be achieved.

More powerful microcomputers and available software packages allow the facility manager to readily examine these alternatives. The logic for the preferred alternative, budget, and schedule should be presented in the rationale. A good logical analysis of the need and the solutions that have been considered is more likely to sell a project than are the correct numbers or technical details.

Computer-assisted planning—developing a program, budget, and schedule—allows the facility manager and his or her consultants to quickly generate different scenarios, each based on different assumptions. Different escalations, finance rates, or costs can be plugged in to assess their impacts on the budget. Similarly, schedules can be manipulated by adding resources, scheduling overtime, or restructuring tasks.

But this new capability and technological advances have had a pernicious impact on the expectations of those we serve—they want fast but correct answers, projects completed yesterday, and speedy efficiency. Good management skills, not only technical expertise, are increasingly required.

This speeding up of the process necessitates that facility managers anticipate as well as respond. They should be tracking products or conducting facilities-related research before projects need the answers from that research. They should be evaluating products; developing in-house databases on costs, user needs, and consultants; and setting up working relationships with end user representatives and decision makers. Other managers need to be educated about how a facility manager can help them, how a design project proceeds. Facility managers want to position themselves as trusted professionals—someone to call when changes to the business occur.

Predesign "simulations" are becoming more common, and more important. Furniture or systems mock-ups, CAD imaging, models or games, and other methods of simulating a new environment are being used to sell or test design concepts. They are also used to promote user acceptance, establish standards, and evaluate the feasibility of a particular solution. Psychological assessments of the corporate culture or user needs and market research techniques or focus groups often document the "soft" or political issues that often must be addressed to make a project successful. These and other new simulation techniques will allow facility managers to analyze the use of, and appropriateness of, a project design as well as its economic feasibility.

5

Interior Design

5.1 Introduction

Interior design is big business. While the facility manager is concentrating on negotiating fees to be under $3 per usable square foot, interior design firms are totaling their income in the millions.

Considering the multitude of staff required by the design firms to satisfy the facility manager, do they make any money? In 1987 Gensler and Associates was the number one interior design giant. Gensler lists 430 people as the total interior design staff employed and 95 staff as nonbillable. Someone is footing the bill.

This is not meant as a complaint. These firms are true extensions of the corporate facility management department. If facility managers have a choice, we would most likely choose to have design done in-house. However, with corporate limitations on staffing, the next best solution is to utilize external consultants to fill this void.

Corporations must fund any staff member with salary, benefits, overhead (rent, etc.) each year. A consultant firm's staff is billed at salary times a multiple calculated to cover the firm's overhead. The corporation capitalizes these costs over the life of the project (usually 5 to 10 years). The tax advantages are in favor of the corporation to follow this philosophy. This is outlined in more detail in this chapter. Facility managers and design principals are aware of this and make the best of the situation.

Each year, I wait for the top 100 (or 200) interior design giants list. This list has appeared in *Interior Design Magazine* and *Corporate Design*. It is interesting to read who's "hot" and who's "not." In reviewing the list for the last 10 years, 1978 to 1987, one can see that some interesting changes have occurred.

Some firms that were big in 1978 are now gone. Other firms have risen to the top and stayed. The latest trend I see is the eventual "elimination" of the middle-size firms. The 1988 giants are those with fees in excess of $15 million and hundreds of staff. The middle-size firms are either buying each other or being bought. P.H.H. Design will be in the top five by 1989 by purchasing four smaller design firms. Others will be following. Design firms are now in the merger mode that corporate America went through in 1986 and 1987. The very small firms, under 30 staff, will continue as speciality service firms.

The number 1 firm in 1987 listed $32.3 million in fees while the number 1 firm in 1978 listed $6.6 million in fees. Even though inflation accounts for some of the change, there is a lot of interior design happening out there! Gensler and Associates was number 13 in 1978 with 3 million square feet of design. In 1987 the firm listed 9.33 million square feet.

What did we, as facility managers, have to give these firms? The statistics for only the top 20 firms are staggering (see Table 5.1).

The costs to provide services are mounting for the facility managers and for the designers. One major design change in the past few years is computer-aided design and drafting.

The computer is here to save all of us time and fees. The computer is here to increase our productivity. This has not yet occurred. Wasn't it the computer that would make us a paperless society? File manufacturers can't turn out files fast enough for us to fill. These gains in productivity may never arrive.

The drama of installing an in-house computer-aided system is still a mysterious desire of senior and middle management. And the consultants are following exactly the same route.

There are many fine books on design and color sense. This book examines the reality of corporate life:

- Should your company invest in CAD?

- If so, what do you analyze?

- How do you go about it?

TABLE 5.1   1987 Corporate Facility Expenditures As Reported by the Top 20 Interior Design Firms

Fees paid to Top 20 interior design firms by corporations	$ 239.8 million
Dollar volume spent by corporations to build or renovate	$3750.1 million
Square footage built by corporations	87.9 million

SOURCE: *Interior Design* list of Top 200 interior design giants report put together by Clifford Pearson with statistical analysis by Andrew Loebelson and statistical compilation by Kathy Harrigan.

- If the corporation is hiring consultants, how do you analyze their CAD?

- If the consultant does not have CAD, how do you hire a design firm?

- What do you ask the design firms?

- What is a fair charge for their services?

These questions and others are answered. Theodore Stout, who helped develop PERFORM,* a sophisticated facility management program put out by Westinghouse, wrote the Words of Others. Ted examines the true corporate viewpoint of CAD and interior design.

5.2 Do It with In-House Computer-Aided Design

In corporations without computer-aided design (CAD), the desire to install such a system sometimes becomes a passion to "keep up with the Joneses" in lieu of true need. This is certainly the wrong approach. The following is a recommended methodology for computerization of facilities management functions.

The five general categories are:

- Computerization suitability analysis
- Applications phase
- Identification phase
- Purchasing phase
- Implementation

Computerization suitability analysis

The facility manager commences the study with the obvious analysis. CAD means to computerize the drafting function. Therefore, the steps are:

- Analyze the drafting productivity of existing staff.

- Analyze the fees expended to hire external architectural and interior design firms.

- Answer the question: What if status quo? Surprisingly, it may show no need to computerize.

---

*PERFORM was released at the annual International Facility Management Association conference in November 1987.

Drafting productivity can be hard to pin down. The facility manager should cover each design activity performed as computed by project size in square feet and complexity. Do not overlook the number of times the same activity is performed. As an example, feasibility portions of a project may require two or three designs while contract documents may require only one.

The drafting and design phases are the most obvious. However, other applications are included in the next area.

Applications phase

Simply review various functions performed by facility management staff for potential computerization. General areas of consideration and their typical applications are:

- Space planning: including stacking plans, block allocation plans, and space inventory information
- Furniture and art purchasing: including tracking of purchase orders, inventory (by person, by workstation, by furniture type, by department), and specifications
- Project scheduling: schedules, payment records, project status reports, timeliness measures
- Design and engineering drawings: master drawing file, increased design production, standardization of drawing appearance, simplified revisions, and reduced errors
- Construction management: quantity takeoffs, accurate estimates, specifications
- Asset management: complete documentation allowing accurate records for tax purposes, depreciation, and write-offs
- Administrative functions: including word-processing functions of editing, graphics, math, organizational charts, spelling, expense tracking, production printing of orders, electronic files and recordkeeping, vendor files, reporting to management, job cost history file

Identification phase

- Define functional needs from applications phase.
- Review available systems. The facility manager should review existing systems that are on the market, talk with current users, and limit the selection to three to five systems.
- Request quotations. Write a clear request for proposal. Review the

received quotation for correctness and adherence to the request for proposal.

- Perform a benchmark (weighted) analysis. This functional evaluation reflects the selected vendors with assigned weight in four major categories: software, support, hardware, and firmware (see Tables 5.2 and 5.3).

- Assign a weight of 10 when using a weighted analysis to your top choice and compare the other vendors in relation to that choice, for that attribute. The facility manager scores the vendors and the extension of their score (weight multiplied by score).

- Total the four attributes on a summary page and average the scores (sum of the extension scores divided by four). The highest score is your recommended vendor (see Table 5.4).

- Perform an economic analysis to analyze the maintenance costs, training costs, prices, and any other pertinent financial information.

- Make a recommendation. Senior management does not choose a system but rather decides whether or not to purchase one.

TABLE 5.2   Yourco, Inc., Computer-Aided Design Functional Evaluation Matrix Software and Support

Attributes	Weight	Vendor A		Vendor B		Vendor C	
		Score	Extension	Score	Extension	Score	Extension
Software							
Architecture	0.35	6	2.10	10	3.50	4	1.40
Report generation	0.35	5	1.75	10	3.50	7	2.45
Engineering	0.10	10	1.00	6	0.60	5	0.50
Space planning	0.10	10	1.00	5	0.50	7	0.70
3rd-party capability	0.05	10	0.50	7	0.35	8	0.40
Communicate to other CAD systems	0.05	10	0.50	7	0.35	10	0.50
Total	1.00		6.85		8.80		5.95
Support							
Software support	0.30	6	1.80	8	2.40	10	1.80
Maintenance	0.20	10	2.00	9	1.80	10	1.20
Training	0.20	8	1.60	10	2.00	7	1.20
Commitment to architecture and engineering	0.10	9	0.90	10	1.00	9	0.60
Company support	0.10	10	1.00	8	0.80	6	0.60
Large user group	0.10	9	0.90	6	0.60	10	0.60
Total	1.00		8.20		8.60		6.00

TABLE 5.3   Yourco, Inc., Computer-Aided Design Functional Evaluation Matrix
Hardware and Firmware

Attributes	Weight	Vendor A		Vendor B		Vendor C	
		Score	Extension	Score	Extension	Score	Extension
Hardware							
Workstation criteria							
Ergonomics	0.40	10	4.00	8	3.20	6	2.40
Intelligence	0.10	6	0.60	8	0.80	10	1.00
Response time under normal operations	0.20	10	2.00	2	0.40	7	1.40
Degradation of CAD with multitasking	0.15	7	1.05	7	1.05	10	1.50
Screen clarity/size	0.10	10	1.00	8	0.80	6	0.60
Environmental needs	0.05	6	0.30	6	0.30	10	0.50
Total	1.00		8.95		6.55		7.40
Firmware							
Power and simplicity							
Graphics	0.40	7	2.80	10	4.00	7	2.80
Easy to use	0.15	10	1.50	6	0.90	10	1.50
Command language	0.12	5	0.60	10	1.20	5	0.60
3-D capabilities	0.03	10	0.30	6	0.18	6	0.18
System management							
Development needs	0.15	5	0.75	10	1.50	5	0.75
Menu functionality	0.10	7	0.70	10	1.00	6	0.60
Data storage	0.05	5	0.25	10	0.50	10	0.50
Total	1.00		6.90		9.28		6.93

TABLE 5.4   Yourco, Inc., Computer-Aided Design Functional Evaluation Matrix
Summary

Attributes	Weight	Vendor A		Vendor B		Vendor C	
		Score	Extension	Score	Extension	Score	Extension
Software total	1.00		6.85		8.80		5.95
Support total	1.00		8.20		8.60		6.00
Hardware total	1.00		8.95		6.55		7.40
Firmware total	1.00		6.90		9.28		6.93
Grand total			30.90		33.23		26.28
Average			7.73		8.31		6.57

- Include a "closure"—a line for the senior manager's concurrence. This becomes the authorization to proceed. It is imperative to secure approval at this time; otherwise, you may have to come back a second time to reexplain the purchase.

Purchasing phase

- Meet with the vendor and finalize your best price and conditions. This is no different from negotiating furniture or design fees. A skilled facility manager should be able to handle this with ease.

- Conduct the actual contract negotiations. This includes having lawyers negotiate the fine print in the standard contract that the vendor will offer. *Computer Contract Negotiations,* by Joseph Auer and Charles E. Harris, covers this field in good detail. The book is written from your side of the negotiating table. This is one of your last chances to have influence over the vendor. The other is during the payment process.

Implementation

This requires analysis and work on the part of the facility manager on several fronts. The basic areas of concern, including brief remarks on what you should be accomplishing, follow.

Staff preparation.   Time to be a psychologist. The staff are unprepared and concerned for their jobs. A facility manager should be keeping the staff informed throughout the entire process, not just when training is about to begin.

Site work.   Prepare an appropriate facilities plan. All too often the "shoemaker goes without shoes" syndrome occurs. That is, the facility manager will waive a need for plans and make "it" happen when the computer really is on the truck dock.

Training.   Complete and publish a training schedule. The systems manager should be trained and be back in the office prior to the delivery of the system. All staff to be trained should be accounted for in the plans.

Database.   Define what will be on the system, what format, when it will be put onto the system, and by whom. As an example, to get a running start on newly trained staff, it is acceptable to utilize a computer service bureau to input your facilities information. This will allow the staff to begin "real work" immediately after training.

Delivery and installation.   Plan for the delivery in advance. Do not allow any key personnel to be on vacation during this phase.

Acceptance.   Plan time for the systems manager to have "hands-on" experience. This break-in time allows the systems manager to test performance of the software, hardware, firmware, and the support of the company. Your acceptance means the final payment is due. Thirty to forty-five days is sufficient acceptance time.

Day-to-day operational plan.   Develop and follow standard operating procedures and menus. It is difficult enough with trained staff to utilize the new computer, and it requires discipline to maintain the integrity of the plans.

Follow-up.   Go back after 12 months—analyze the results of the computer installation. The analysis should answer some of the following questions:

- Were those productivity estimates achieved?
- Were the promised head-count reductions achieved?
- What was the final cost compared with the original capital expenditure plan?
- Is the department better off now with the computer than it was prior to its existence?

Pitfalls to avoid

Following the previously outlined procedures should have enabled you to have purchased and installed a fairly respectable system. However, after 6 months of having a system up and running, you begin to have some second thoughts on the choice of the system. These concerns can be traced back to one or more of four areas:

- The salesperson's pitch
- Acquisition tricks
- Installation errors
- Real work begins

The salesperson's pitch.   Be a Doubting Thomas!

- Do not believe the salesperson's pitch unless you can actually see the system work.
- Do not believe the system even after you see it work. Systems can be

rigged to show faster response time than actually exists during multitasking or in cases of adding additional workstations to the system. I recommend visiting current users with systems similar in size to the one you are planning on acquiring.

- Do not believe the term "new generation." This is commonly known as the salesperson's inability to tell you when the system will be in production. Additionally, you should realize that there are no current users. You don't have to be the first one with the new system.

- Do not believe the term "office environment compatible." Experienced CAD users realize this means that special air-conditioning and lighting are probably still required despite the salesperson's disclaimers.

- Do not believe in the standard vendor-demonstrated programs. They *always* work well. While the prospective system can do all work, can it do your work? I recommend you overcome this by writing a benchmark. A benchmark is one or more typical examples of the work you expect to perform on the system. Have this work actually drawn/performed by the CAD system.

- Do not believe the term "immediate delivery." This is a sign that you should exercise caution.

- Do not believe the line "The system is immediately usable without any kind of modification." The perfect system for any user does not exist. Either you change the way business is done to meet the demands of the system or expect to accomplish some customization.

- Do not let the salesperson meet your senior manager. The standard productivity ratio gains of 3 or 4 to 1 are very attractive to the budget-minded supervisor. Those gains are hard to achieve. A facility manager would be satisfied with productivity 2 to 1!

Acquisition tricks.   When going through the acquisition phase of this complex data-processing transaction, be aware of the following:

- Always tell the favored vendor (during the prenegotiating sessions)—without any reservations—that another vendor is under consideration. If you tip your hand, your leverage is gone forever.

- Plan on doing your own daily support to make the system work. The vendor's agreement will always provide for support. While this commitment is made in goodwill, it is just not always possible.

- Make sure you have accounted for this staff time in your initial analysis of real costs to purchase the CAD system.

- Plan on changing the standard vendor agreement, which is 100 percent pro-vendor. Try to maximize deviations from the normal agreement. After all, the larger your corporation is, the more you will probably spend. You know it; they know it; the vendor needs your business; and your lawyers, involved from the beginning, are smart too.

■ Provide for a 30- to 45-day testing and acceptance period, in writing, in the contract. There should be no final payment until after satisfactory completion of this period.

■ Plan your negotiations session in advance. Write down your key points, goals, and expectations. Then, go into the meeting and achieve them!

Installation errors. This is potentially the most embarrassing phase. While you are paying attention to every detail for other projects, the one under your own nose seems to slip. Don't overlook your own CAD installation.

■ Complete your space or room before the scheduled delivery date. There will be enough pressure on you and your staff to be productive immediately. No sense increasing that burden by having the CAD sit in a box waiting for your own construction to be completed.

■ Make sure your test period commences *after* installation, not after the delivery date. Do not plan on such tight timing for room completion that only having the computer delivery delayed will save your job.

■ Do not rely on your local electrician to wire the system without the CAD vendor's support.

■ Plan for flexibility both in your furniture layout and in your lighting plan. Only when the CAD system is installed and the workstation used will you appreciate the ability to make changes needed because of glare or ergonomics.

■ Train your systems operator or any staff that tests the system *prior* to installation. It may take up to 8 work days for the full training on the system for *each* staff member. This is not part of the test-and-acceptance time clock.

■ Do not plan to train the balance of staff *and* use the same workstation(s) for previously trained staff at the same time. It may pay to invest in fully training all the staff just prior to the system's installation.

■ Do not overlook the psychological aspect. Do not be too surprised to lose at least 10 percent of your staff. The reasons include concerns about job security, opportunities to sell their newly learned skills (to another firm), or resistance to the change.

Real work begins.   The system has been installed, tested, and accepted. Now it is time for real work to begin. Now what?

- Establish your departmental standard operating procedures for inputting information onto the CAD prior to the real work. Standard menus, formatting, and other detailed items should be published to the staff.

- Plan where information is to be stored. The CAD system has 64 or more layers available for storing information. The CAD vendor personnel can be invaluable in planning for this.

- Program your base-building information into the CAD. Even if you have trained your staff and are ready to work, what will you work on? A significant amount of time is required to put your base-building plans onto the system. If you start to input this information only after acceptance, you'll never come close to your productivity goals.

  It may be worth the investment to have a CAD service bureau do the inputting just prior to delivery. These service bureaus have the same system and give you a quick start after installation. Additionally, if extra staff is required for a large project, the bureau can supply staff at an hourly rate without your having to hire new in-house staff.

- Do not throw out the drawing boards, pens, pencils, triangles, erasers, or straightedges. Your staff will continue to use both the manual and electronic methods. The CAD system is another tool for them.

- Consider multiple shifts of staff if work load exceeds CAD availability time. Productivity levels are difficult to reach on a 9-to-5 day. The staff may not like this approach.

- Have a regular maintenance schedule. Virtually all systems are sold with maintenance as part of the purchase package.

Summary

Proper planning, skillful purchasing, and timely staff involvement will lead to a successful start of an in-house CAD system. It takes plenty of time and effort to get to this point. It takes even more time and patience to have day-to-day success with the system. In addition to the tips and pitfalls, a commonsense approach helps you get the most out of the system and your staff.

If the analysis reflects that a computer-aided system is not to be, or senior management turns down the purchase—it's okay. Make the best of existing staff. You can revisit the purchase issue at a future date. Management attitudes and financial conditions change.

5.3 Do It with External Consultants

Facility managers want to be reassured that any CAD system they get with the external design consultant they hire is world-famous.

Facility managers want the design firm's system to plan, manage, and remember all the corporate schemes. Facility managers want a system that can monitor all projects. Facility managers want a system that tracks all their expenses. The system must be able to maintain an instantly accessible and retrievable information base. A system that is productive, effective, and efficient. Facility managers do not expect to pay extra for any of these attributes.

A recent advertisement outlined a seemingly excellent system. The text read: "This world-famous self-management plan-manage-memory system offers you a quantum leap in increased executive productivity, effectiveness, and efficiency." However, this system used no electricity. This advertisement for Day-Timers desk and pocket calendars sounds exactly like a pitch from a design firm hawking their in-house CAD system. With a Day-Timer costing about $20, that would buy about 20 minutes of CPU time on the consultant's CAD.

A design firm buys a computer for various reasons and uses during the project life cycle. The CAD system starts as one of the marketing tools to dazzle the facility manager. The system will contribute immediately to the project by its use in programming, feasibility studies, and cost estimates.

The system continues as a vital design tool throughout:

- Schematic design phase
- Design development
- Contract or construction documents
- Bidding documents
- Construction phases
- Scheduling throughout the project
- Follow-up churn and maintenance
- Ongoing lease information

Each of these phases can have many subcategories that the design firm performs on the CAD. As an example, the feasibility phase could include active computer-aided design for the following:

- Strategic planning
- Space planning
- Space inventory
- Space allocations
- Space management
- Site planning
- Three-dimensional modeling
- Building massing
- Budgets
- Scheduling
- Adjacency and spatial requirements
- Stacking plans
- Programming information, including staff projections
- Block diagrams

The external design firm is most likely to invest in the various software available to be able to accomplish any and all of the tasks at hand.

Selecting the right consultant

Facility managers need to know how to interview the design consultant insofar as CAD availability is concerned. You need to start with an assessment of your own internal system, whether it is manual or electronic.

- How does your corporation work?
- What are your standards?
- What type of drawings are required?
- What will you do with an electronic file?

Once you are comfortable with your firm's answers to these questions, bring on the design firms. The interview process includes a series of questions to be posed to the design firm in the following categories: experience, attributes, and costs.

- Experience
  - What is the design firm's experience with the CAD system?
  - How long have their designers had the system running?
  - What are the levels of complexity of the projects already completed on the CAD?
  - Have they done any projects relatively similar to the project at hand?
  - Do not overlook the importance of talking to the actual staff of the design firm who will operate the CAD.
  - What is the professionalism of the designer's staff who will be assigned to the project?
  - Are their staff trained as CAD operators or designers?
  - Are these staff people the same staff that designed the projects the design firm is showing as samples of their best work?
  - Does the design firm use a CAD service bureau?

- Attributes
  - Since this system is world-famous, what does it *not* have?
  - How often is the system down?
  - When the system is down, what contingency plans does the firm have to complete the work?
  - Does a service bureau back up the firm? If so, are there any hidden extra costs?
  - Does the CAD vendor continue to support the system?
  - Who does the maintenance on the system?
  - If this CAD system is not world-famous, is it compatible with your own system?
  - What special features are in this system that do *not* support the facility manager's own internal standards?
  - Is this system a hodgepodge of various off-the-shelf components? If every manufacturer has a piece of the action, then how does the designer back it up?
  - If the software is so specialized, will you be tied in to this firm's system forever?

- Costs
  - What does it cost? is *not* your next question.
  - What is standard on the system? What furniture systems are already programmed into the system? This may actually reduce your production drawing costs.
  - What does the built-in specification and hardware schedule look like? It may be cost-effective to utilize the designer's schedules in lieu of your own standards.

There are three basic ways that the design firm will quote prices to a facility manager.

- Percentage of project costs
- Lump-sum basis
- Cost per square foot

Percentage. This method is quite simple to calculate. Designers figure that a certain percentage of any given project will cover all firm personnel costs and allow for sufficient profit. Therefore, a $1 million project quoted at 8 percent will result in a fee of $80,000.

If you control project costs, you will know the full cost of the designer, and there should be no further expenditures. Design firms have sufficient experience with other projects to have faith that the percentage will handle their complete staff's involvement.

A disadvantage is that if the project is miscalculated, the designer needs to ask for more funding or scale back on the project coverage. A disadvantage for the facility manager is the concern that if the design fee is tied into the project cost, there is no incentive for the designer to save on expenses. The more expensive the level of construction finishes, the furniture system (wood instead of steel), or floor covering, the more the 8 percent fee is multiplied by. The monthly or periodic billing under this method can also be frustrating for the facility manager. Since the percentage is based on the final costs, and there are no costs until well into the project, how does the designer invoice?

Usually, the fees are broken into percentage by project phase. Each phase then is estimated to last a specific number of weeks or months and the fee is billed evenly. An example of the 8 percent fee on that $1 million project is shown in Table 5.5.

I do not recommend this method. There are too many variables on a project to give you a comfortable feeling on the final fee. Furthermore, during the many weeks of the project, facility managers find themselves approving invoices based on percentages without necessarily seeing a corresponding amount of work being performed.

There is an uneasiness in watching every specification done by the designer. The realization that the designer's best interests of higher costs mean higher fees is in direct conflict with the facility manager's goals of cost reduction.

The percentage method is seldom utilized for interior design projects. If a project is canceled when it is partially designed, what is the percentage based upon?

TABLE 5.5   Yourco, Inc., Percentage Fee Calculation

Phase	Percent	Fee ($)	Duration (weeks)
Programming	5	4,000	3
Feasibility	10	8,000	6
Design development	25	20,000	6
Contract documents	40	32,000	12
Bidding	3	2,400	3
Construction	15	12,000	16
Move-in/punchlist	2	1,600	4
Totals	100	80,000	50

Lump-sum basis. Under the lump-sum method, the designer responds to your quotation request with a single dollar amount. Using the sample project above, the designer might respond with a fee quote of $80,000. The designer would also estimate the project life at 50 weeks or 11.5 months, with 11 equal payments of $6950 per month, and the final payment to be prorated.

Your advantage is that the costs are known up front. If the project proceeds without any changes, then the price is set. The designer's advantage is that all costs to complete this project with a reasonable profit are included. If the project is canceled, the designer's disadvantage may be that more staff time was expended than actual fee received.

The designer's best interests are served by getting the project done as quickly as possible. This reduces actual staff time spent and maximizes the profit since the upper limit of the fee is fixed.

Your disadvantages are that there is no basis of the amount of time any of the design staff spends on the project. If the project is canceled, then possibly a disproportionate amount of fee may have been paid. The burden is upon you to ensure that the initial design contract is very explicit on the amount and level of services included in the design fees. Extra services will be at an hourly rate, which considerably changes the expected fees.

The only win—win issue is that the facility manager and the designer want the project design done as quickly as possible. I don't recommend this method. The negative aspects outweigh the positive ones. The facility manager becomes a watchdog to ensure that the designer performs the full level of services under the contract. The designer becomes a watchdog to make sure that you do not keep adding small extras without adding to the base fee. This method does not promote a team approach to the basic goal of completing the project.

Cost per square foot.   There should be no doubt that for interior design projects the common denominator is *usable* square feet. Do not use rentable square feet or gross square feet. The design firm has been performing good, competent design services for an average $3 per usable square foot (USF). The design firm purchases a CAD system to:

- Expedite their design work.
- Ensure more accurate work and specifications.
- Improve their design.
- Speed up their production turnaround time.
- Increase staff productivity.

For some reason, the design firms feel they must get their CAD investment back. Therefore, many design firms impose an hourly charge of $50 to 60 per hour for computer time and up to $35 per hour for the operator's time. Something is wrong. Why should you be subjected to extra fees? If productivity is at least 2 to 1, why not charge $1.50 per USF? Why charge for the CAD operator since there should be far less manual drafting time?

At this time, most facility managers resolve the issue with the cost per USF remaining the same, and no further charges for CAD usage. On larger jobs, the CAD will be used (if the firm has one) at the negotiated cost per square foot. Once the CAD issue is settled, what does it mean to use the cost per square foot method? Designers calculate all expected levels of involvement from the staff (time and salary), add the profit factor, and divide by the usable square feet. The designer's percent of profit remains whether the project size increases or decreases.

The facility manager requests that the billing under this method be done on an hourly basis toward the cost per square foot as a not-to-exceed amount. Simply put, a designer's salary ($20.00 per hour) is multiplied by a factor which covers benefits and overhead (industry average 3.25) to arrive at a billable rate ($65.00 per hour). Larger corporations may be able to limit the multiple to 3.0 times direct salary. The sum of all the billable hours is applied each billing period toward the total project fee (USF times cost per square foot).

Each month the project manager only has to pay for the exact number of hours any design firm's staff actually spent on the project. The designer has the same ratio of profit built into each hour worked. The

TABLE 5.6   Yourco, Inc., Fee Estimate Matrix

Project size	Usable square feet	Customer contact	General office	Computer facilities
Small	Under 5000	Cost per square foot price range	Cost per square foot price range	Cost per square foot price range
Intermediate	5001–15,000	Cost per square foot price range	Cost per square foot price range	Cost per square foot price range
Moderate	15,001–25,000	Cost per square foot price range	Cost per square foot price range	Cost per square foot price range
Large	25,000–75,000	Cost per square foot price range	Cost per square foot price range	Cost per square foot price range
Very large	Over 75,000	Negotiable	Negotiable	Negotiable

designer's fee is not tied into the level of finishes or amount of dollars spent. The team members can both work toward a cost-effective design solution.

You can further reduce time in the beginning of a project by getting estimated fee ranges from a designer on an annual cycle. There would be no commitment from you to hire the firm, but they would be expected to perform their services within the fee ranges. A sample fee estimate matrix that your designer might submit is shown in Table 5.6.

I recommend this method. The cost per square foot method with the total fee serving as a not-to-exceed limit is the best way to employ design firms. In this case, both the facility manager and the designer are on the same side of the project's goals, and the advantages for both sides far outweigh the negatives.

Summary

The design firm's CAD is only their tool, not their only tool. The designers most important products are their people. Their staff:

- Are the ones that interview your senior managers
- Manage the utilization of the CAD
- Make the presentations to the facility manager
- Interpret the findings
- Participate at midnight during the move-in

If the CAD is the only thing you like about a design firm, forget them and buy the Day-Timer instead. If you have confidence in the design firm's people, the decision is made. It is not unusual for design firms to have 5- to 10-year relationships with corporations. Designer's staff become almost like employees with their in-depth knowledge of the workings of the corporation and their constant on-site presence.

If the facility manager and the design firm have CAD systems that interface, the relationship is further enhanced through on-line updates between systems. External architectural, interior, and engineering design consultants are extensions of the in-house facility team. The possibility of electronic connections serves to help you respond faster and more accurately to senior management requests.

5.4   The Words of Others—Computer-Aided Design

Theodore B. Stout   *President, Resource
Sciences Associates, Inc.*

Monday, 8:37 a.m. The corporate boardroom of the Very Big, Gigantic Mega-Corporation of America Company, Ltd.:

"Cream?"

"No thanks. I think I'll pass on the coffee too. This morning's bran has my stomach all in knots."

"Yeah. I know what you mean. My wife's got me on the bran kick too. I must admit, I do feel better."

"Me too, but the mornings are hell. So, what's on the agenda this morning?"

"Well, let's see. We have Anderson on the new mining investments, Jacobs on the new marketing plan, Watson on the overseas investments, and, ah yes, they always save the best for the last."

"Not the new building again?"

"Yup. Never have been able to figure out what they're talking about. Just seems like they want to spend money."

"Yeah, but have you seen the pictures and colors for the new executive dining room?"

"Just keep your mind on the building, if that's possible."

"What? Floor plans?"

"Yeah, floor plans. I never have figured out how to read them."

"Me neither. I still remember last year when my wife put that addition onto the house. She kept on showing me floor plans and wanting me to approve them. So I did. All I know is that I spent 200 grand and got a warm place to, ah, read my paper."

"Ever since these guys got that computer we now have four times as many floor plans to look at. It's like the guys in accounting that used to get spread-sheetitis once they got that new financial program. Glad we put a stop to that. Financial projections 30 years out! Come on!"

"But at least we got some data that related to the company's current and future financial positions. It would help with making more realistic decisions if we got some of the same stuff from the facility management group."

"Now wait a minute. We do get budget and other financial information from the facilities group."

"You don't understand. This whole discussion began because of computers. At least there was a modicum of restraint of drawing proliferation when we used that outside space planning firm and their computer-aided design system. Our own facilities group only had a PC and was constrained to project management and budgeting."

"Now look at us. Ever since we brought the CAD capability in-house there has been no restraint! And I have never seen a report on how we actually achieved any economies or increased productivity."

"We are one of the most so-called computer-literate companies in the United States. What does that get us? More floor plans! Not better financials, not better operations projections, not better resource controls, just more floor plans."

"I keep on feeling that the reason we bought 2200 ergo-whatsit chairs last year was not because of the financial justification that they would increase productivity, but because the chair fabric color matched the new carpet color."

"They do look nice."

"That's not the point! Why can't we get the same depth of corporate and financial information from the facilities group that we get from every other group? I mean, look at the amount of money we spend each year to manage data about ourselves. Why can't we use that computer power to help us better manage our facilities and other resources, not just generate more and better floor plans? If we would have kept the CAD capability separate from the resource data, and put more emphasis on that capability, we would be in much better control by now."

"What's the difference? It's just interior design."

"It's not just interior design! Everything we do takes place in buildings, especially your departments. The allocation and management of all our resources! People, equipment, machines, furniture, computers—everything. And how it is used directly affects our company's profits."

"I can see you have strong feelings about this."

"I just can't help but think that we are missing a tremendous opportunity here. We need the computers to give us fewer drawings and more information about our resources and their performance. It's as simple as that. If we had that information, it would give us a control over our operations that we have never had before, and it could help us make better decisions, both short- and long-term. We might even be able to understand the productivity issue and how it affects our bottom line."

"Just what in-flight magazines have you been reading lately?"

"You just don't get it, do you? The mind-set about these types of things around here never ceases to amaze me. We have all this computer power, and no one can even tell me what our lease liability is. But we have umpteen levels of floor plans of every slop closet of every building we have ever looked at! Amazing, simply amazing.

"Oh, well. Obviously our major challenge here is not to think strategically but to think horizontally."

"I'm not quite sure what that means, and I probably should resent it, but I won't. Come on, Jeff. Once the building's done and you get into that new corner office overlooking the river, you'll be able to focus more on the work you're so good at: corporate takeovers."

"Yeah, I guess you're right, Mike. Maybe I'll even take a course on reading floor plans. That way I'll at least know what corner of the building I'm in."

"Good morning Jeff, Michael."

"Good morning R. J."

"Morning, R. J."

"Cream, R. J.?"

"No thanks. I think I'll pass on the coffee too. This morning's bran has my stomach all in knots. What's on the agenda?"

"Anderson and the mining deal. Jacobs is going to review the new marketing plan, Watson on the overseas investments, and then we have another building review."

"Great! Are they going to have the pictures and colors for the new executive dining room?"

And so the story goes: how much, what kind, and for what—does corporate America even need facility information? And does it even care? In most cases, organizations don't even realize the area of productivity opportunity that exists. But the computer can be the key not only to the identification and successful management of these opportunities but to the strategic positioning of facilities management within the organization.

In the past, the currency of power was information. Paper was passed up the corporate ladder until finally one individual, the "boss," made a decision. The closer you were to the boss, the more people that were passing paper to you, and the more powerful you were.

Today, most of the information that used to reach the boss is available at the press of a computer key, in full color graphics. Today, the currency of power is not the *accumulation* of information but rather the *use* of information. Information is now available at the level where the results of a decision will be witnessed. The feedback loop involving information, decision, and result is more immediate and more visible.

The computer, combined with ongoing societal shifts, combined with new management approaches, combined with a competitive business world has yielded a new manner of doing work, and an alternative format for the facility manager.

The facility manager has access to more data about the organization to do his or her job than any other individual. Either computers can be utilized to gain minor efficiencies in the processing of this data (either floor plans or strategic facility plan) or they can assist in the positioning of the facility management function within the organization through the more adroit and strategic use of information.

In-house or out-of-house computer-aided design capabilities have never been the real issue, for the real potential exists in *how,* not *how much* the facility manager uses information. Computers can either enhance or diminish this process.

6

Furniture Management

6.1 Introduction

Twenty years' experience in purchasing furniture is absolutely essential prior to having your first negotiation session with a national vendor. While this is virtually impossible to achieve, with the tips in this chapter you may be able to add a few years to your background.

Furniture manufacturers and vendors—all anxious to have your order and equally interested in having your continued business—really nurture a long-term relationship with the facility manager. I encourage the facility manager to take full advantage of this fact. Small-time users of furniture may never get the opportunity again.

Large users get tired of the constant marketing. My experience with open plan furniture includes purchasing and installing over three million square feet of Steelcase products and another three million square feet of Herman Miller products. These two furniture companies are about the best in management philosophy and style.

Steelcase remains far larger and far ahead in many aspects of customer relationships. In July 1987, I was invited to give my views of dealing with Herman Miller. I spoke in front of the chairman and his management team, about 150 people, and the speech was broadcast live to all their offices around the country.

As an introduction to this section, here are some excerpts from that speech, "Furniture and the Facility Manager."

> As the story goes, an accountant, a furniture manufacturer's representative, and a facility manager went on safari. Cannibals captured them. As the pots were boiling, the chief of the tribe came to each one, and said he would grant them one final wish before they died!
>
> The accountant asked that he be allowed to balance his financial accounts before he met his maker. The request would be granted, the chief said.

The furniture representative asked that he be allowed, before he died, to give a speech on the history of his company from the company's very beginnings out of the founder's garage, through the days of innovative design in the sixties, and how today's successful line is marketed through a dozen regional offices. This too would be granted, said the chief.

The chief then asked the facility manager what his last wish was. The facility manager said, "Kill me right *now*. I've heard that furniture speech six times already."

I am constantly marketed by all furniture manufacturers. I certainly welcome the opportunity to reverse the trend to discuss a facility manager's perceptions.

The excellent 1986 annual report covered answers to questions a facility manager always wanted to know. Here are a few that were missed in the report about my company:

Item	Number
National furniture purchasing agreement	4
Surplus furniture items reused out of warehouse	9957
Projects last year over $25,000	281
Average phone calls I receive each day	62
Approximate square feet occupied	25 million
Single largest project	New 50-story building
Single smallest project	250 business cards
Furniture purchase orders issued in a year	5000

All the statistics reflected a busy organization with lots of change and churn. The basic goal is that we must plan flexibility into our space standards and furniture systems to accommodate future changes in technology and in our businesses.

Flexibility means systems will be moved around, be raised and lowered, wired, rewired, assembled and disassembled. You'll remember the movie *Short Circuit* from 1986. This featured a robot named Number Five. The robot discovered that the term "disassemble" meant death. I can assure Number Five that due to our churn and renovation rate of 25 percent all our disassembled furniture has a new life as reassembled workstations elsewhere in one of our facilities.

We hope that all our vendors will provide us with the maximum flexibility and ease of disassembly/reassembly. I know it is your goal and it will be greatly welcomed when it arrives.

Finally, I would like to discuss the end user's perception of Herman Miller. The press articles are all favorable, including the feeling of a happy family atmosphere. While you receive many visitors here in Michigan, how many of you have visited an actual installation in New York?

What happens between Michigan and the user move-in? A user cannot understand why items take eight or more weeks to deliver. And then when a large order arrives, certain pieces are missing, damaged, or otherwise not correct. In some cases, it is the facility manager's fault, in other cases, it is the dealer, and in some it is the manufacturer. Why should an item that you spent so much time manufacturing, assembling, stapling, packing, and shipping arrive damaged?

The hottest item in the marketplace is Ethospace. I recently had a four-person mock-up put up in my office area, including my own office. Why does it take four hundred boxes for just four offices?

Why not shrink-wrap?

Why are there bar codes on the individual boxes which help you deliver when these boxes are discarded? Why not bar-code the individual pieces to help us inventory?

How do I store the excess pieces? Have any stacking devices been developed?

We know a good product when we see one. We are not interested in fly-by-night firms that will not continue our chosen colors, fabrics or sizes. We deal with firms that value integrity and take pride in their work. We deal with firms that value customer satisfaction. We also deal with firms that give us the best buy for our corporate dollar.

A five-year national purchasing agreement is a great achievement for your firm. What it means to us is that we are dealing with a company that has a proven record of continuous service, products, and reliable dealers.

We have been dealing with Herman Miller since 1968, and we see no reason to change at this point.

The next time you are on safari and you get captured. You can tell that tribal chief that your last wish has been fulfilled—you finally met a satisfied customer.

While this speech had some humor, it covered the essential reasons to have national contracts. The pride of the worker, the integrity of the company, and quality workmanship are what the facility manager expects when issuing a purchase order. Our allegiance is consistently with the best buy from a quality firm.

The chapter examines a sample national furniture agreement, the purchase order process, and managing the big move-in. One manner to evaluate the success of the move is also discussed—the post-occupancy evaluation.

6.2   Think Big: The National Contract

The national contract has great advantages for the facility manager: good pricing, better service, reliability of product lines and finishes, and the elimination of bidding each and every furniture purchase. The argument that a standard furniture selection leads to stale space gets too little credit from facility managers. Buying one type of furniture in one color or finish can be deadly, but furniture manufacturers have moved far beyond this stage. Larger manufacturers now buy smaller manufacturers, to the facility manager's delight for the following reasons:

- One-stop shopping reduces dealing with vendors on a project to a handful.
- Negotiating for a family discount from the combined manufacturer's product line becomes possible.
- The opportunity to get exact color and finishes on products that previously only blended improves their look.
- There is reliability on the continuance of products.

Leasing

While this chapter covers the terms of a national contract, it is important that the facility manager realize that leasing provides an alternative to purchasing.

Many firms lease airplanes, oil tankers, equipment, office spaces, and even their employees (from temporary agencies). Why not lease the furniture and eliminate the need to capitalize? The facility manager could lease it through a leasing company that would buy the furniture through the same dealer the facility managers uses.

Using the same dealer accounts for guaranteed service levels that previously satisfied the facility manager. When the lease is up, the furniture magically disappears without the concerns of storage, sales, or dumping.

The basic leases available include:

1. *Lease with an option to buy.* This method entails a lease for a specific time period. At the end of the leasing period, the facility manager can renew the lease, return the furniture for new or updated items, or buy it. The purchase price of the furniture, usually negotiated at the origination of the lease, will be reduced by the rental payments previously paid.

2. *Straight lease.* A normal lease agreement, like office space, can be fixed for a long term or last an indefinite time by providing unlimited renewals. The ownership rests with the leasing company. There are no property taxes to pay or depreciation expenses to be accounted.

The national contract defined

The national purchase agreement with a manufacturer can cover the leasing option. It is basically transparent to the vendor if the leasing company or the end user owns the furniture. In either case, the sale has been made.

Listed below are principal clauses that should be included in a national purchasing agreement with the manufacturer. There are two basic agreements that one can follow: two-party agreement or three-party agreement. The two-party pact is between the corporation and one of the following two: the manufacturer or the dealer.

1. *Two-party agreement: Corporation and manufacturer.* The contract with the manufacturer will be a direct purchase agreement and does not initially account for the installation. Facility managers with in-house crews will opt for this method because the dealer is not required for installation or servicing.

Facility managers without in-house crews can still utilize this format. The installation costs will be negotiated directly with the dealer, and the smart facility manager will use the leverage of the manufacturer to get better pricing.

Facility managers should be aware that installations must be in accordance with manufacturer's standards and specifications to maintain warranty coverage. The pricing will be at a higher discount because the dealer installation cost will *not* be included. This is known as drop ship pricing.

2. *Two-party agreement: Corporation and dealer.* The contract with the dealer will be an indirect purchase of the manufacturer's product but it guarantees that when the corporation does purchase furniture, it will only be through the dealer.

The facility manager will have a lower discount off the list price since the contract will normally include the cost of installation. Drop ship pricing is still a viable solution, with the installation price negotiated separately and included in the contract.

This form of contract is used by facility managers who have no in-house crew available, or by those who do not care to deal with the manufacturer on every order. The facility manager can use this format to have all nationwide projects managed by the single dealer.This format can also be used to have the dealer act as the core of a network of dealers. This way the facility manager deals with the large network dealer that is domiciled in the facility manager's town.

3. *Three-party agreement: Corporation, manufacturer, and dealer.* This contract is signed by all three parties. This form assures the facility manager that the manufacturer will support the dealer. The facility manager is relieved of managing either the manufacturer or the dealer, as in a two-party agreement. The manufacturers might seek to avoid this format since

they would prefer selling to the dealer or to the corporation without further responsibilities.

The facility manager negotiates pricing with the manufacturer for product and with the dealer for installations. This makes manufacturer, dealer, and corporation all part of the team for a successful project. This agreement normally eliminates conflicts among the parties.

Drop ship pricing and other special pricing packages are still included.

The national contract terms

The national agreement should cover the following points:

- Basic agreement
- Purchasing definitions
- Invoicing terms
- Shipping terms
- Delivery and installation procedures and terms
- Acceptance and inspection
- Title and claims
- Account representation
- Warranties and indemnities
- Legal and regulatory terms
- Pricing definitions and terms
- Dealers

Example agreement. This example is based on the facility manager's negotiating a two-party agreement between the manufacturer and the corporation (called Yourco in this example) with the dealer as a named resource in the contract but not a signer.

1 Agreement

Parties	Agreement between Yourco and Manufacturer
Boundary	Continental United States and Puerto Rico
Purpose	To use reasonable efforts to purchase the manufacturer's products
Period	Suggest 3 to 5 years
Terminate	90 days advance notice by either party

Entirety	Nothing else written by parties can change this agreement
Assignment	Yourco can assign contract to subsidiaries, Manufacturer only to subcontractors
Notices	Definition of acceptable notice delivery, including name of contacts for parties

2 Purchasing

Orders	In writing, dated, with delivery and price terms, right to change delivery location
Price	Per Manufacturer price book dated _____
Changes	Price increases on 30/60/90/120 days notice (get the best deferrment you can negotiate)
New items	New products to be priced within 90 days
Cancel	Cancellation terms tied into order size, specials, warehouse stock, quick ship, and noncatalog specials not cancelable

3 Invoicing

Timing	Invoices may be received any time after the ship date, payment within 30 working days after installation (or after delivery if you cannot get from installation).
Method	Payment is to be by corporate check, not cash.
Delays	Pay only 90 percent of cost.
Taxes	Yourco will pay all applicable taxes after discount is applied to list price.

4 Shipping

Freight	There are to be no charges beyond minimal dollar order quantity.
Labels	Manufacturer will label or tag each carton with Yourco name, address, floor, facility manager's name.
Packing	Special packing will be subject to extra charges.
Claims	Dealer is responsible for filing freight claims.

5 Delivery and Installation

Delivery	Manufacturer will do its best to meet dates and dealer will deliver during Yourco's normal business hours, overtime delivery to be estimated in advance.

Notice	There will be 24 to 48 hours advance notification prior to delivery.
Drop ship	Dealer will receive and inspect drop ship products.
Minority	Manufacturer will use reasonable efforts to permit qualified minority-owned vendors to participate in delivery or service subcontracts.
Install	Manufacturer will install furniture at time of delivery, level files, attach all furniture, and remove debris and cartons to a designated area. Electrical work is part of the installation price except where labor trades other than dealer crew are required by local codes.
Insurance	Worker's compensation, property damage, public liability, etc., are dealer expenses and must be a minimum of $1 million. Dealer indemnifies Yourco against any claim or lawsuit that results from negligence of any employee of the dealer.

6 Acceptance and inspection

Inspection	Yourco will have at least 5 working days after installation to inspect furniture.
Rejections	Yourco may reject any item that is found to be defective, damaged, or nonconforming to the original purchase order.
Acceptance	If not rejected, items are deemed to be accepted by Yourco.
Replace	Dealer will repair or replace damaged goods within 1 month.
Risks	Dealer is to bear all risk of loss for any rejected item and is responsible for all handling, and delivery expenses.

7 Title and claims

Title	Items are delivered to Yourco free of any liens, encumbrances, claims, etc. Title passes upon delivery to Yourco.

8 Account representation

Manager	Dealer will designate an employee to act as an account manager to Yourco to oversee the purchase orders, processing thereof, and installations, at no cost to Yourco.
Training	Manufacturer and/or dealer will provide Yourco technical assistance, instructions, and training as required without charge.

9 Warranties and indemnities

Warranty	Items will be good quality; combustion toxicity must meet the Business Industrial Furniture Manufacturer's Association (BIFMA) standards, merchantable quality.
Coverage	Try for 10 years, accept 5 years on base furniture, 5 years on operating and functional mechanisms, 3 years on electrical components. After all, why should you spend so much on furniture if manufacturer does not stand behind its products?
Indemnity	Manufacturer indemnifies Yourco against any liabilities, penalties, etc., incurred by Yourco from any breach of warranty.
Subsidiary	Warranties extend to all subsidiaries of Yourco.
Patents	Manufacturer guarantees products of any patent infringements and indemnifies Yourco.

10 Legal and regulatory

Laws	Manufacturer will comply with local, state, and federal laws and regulations, Yourco's state law is the governing law.
Ads	Manufacturer shall not advertise without Yourco's prior written permission.
Confidential	Both parties are to safeguard confidentiality of information obtained in the course of business.
Ethics	No payments are to be made to anyone pertaining to the agreement or any business between the two parties.
Labor acts	Manufacturer will comply with all federal equal employment opportunity and labor acts.
Act of God	Neither party is at fault for acts of God, war, riots, storm, flood, etc.

11 Pricing

Discounts	All discount percentages are off list price and include delivery and installation.
Orders	Items are ordered at one time to one location.
Project order	Quantity of items is to be shipped to one location covering one project over agreed period of time (phased installations).
Negotiable	Price is to be agreed upon between Yourco and Manufacturer, but no less than best discount.
Leasing	Yourco may lease or purchase furniture at its option; all contract terms remain the same.

Pricing schedule ($)	Product lines (%)		
	A	B	C
0 to 250,000	45	47	49
250,000 to 500,000	47	49	51
500,000 to 750,000	49	51	Neg
Over 750,000		Negotiable	

12 Dealers

Dealers   Dealers named herein are authorized to sell Manufacturer's products at above discounts.

Town(s)   List each dealer that Manufacturer and Yourco have approved; include address, telephone number, principals, contacts.

The national contract is a step into the big time, even for the smallest corporations. Seek out the best furniture lines, meet with the manufacturer and/or dealer, start the relationship.

6.3   The Purchase Order Process

There is nothing more miserable in the facility manager's life than trying to track that one last missing furniture piece.

The one last piece that completes the jigsaw puzzle of a renovation. The one last piece that gets the user to stop calling with the famous line: "Where's my furniture?" The one last piece that was "shipped last Thursday and it should have been there already."

There is a light at the end of the facility tunnel. There is a saving grace. The facility manager has an out. The furniture buyer is there to work out these issues! While it is true the responsibility is with the facility manager, the buyer has the job to negotiate, order, and track the furniture. Let the buyer beware.

In reality, if the furniture buyer has been doing the job properly, then there should be no surprises at the end of the project.

Some corporations don't see the natural working relationship that is essential for a smooth operation of a facilities department. The facility management and the furniture purchasing departments should be within the same area.

When the furniture buyer reports to another department, the priorities get lost with ordering No. 2 pencils. The professional buyer should be concentrating on the big dollar costs of furniture and office equipment purchases. The secretary is quite capable of handling office supplies, including pencils.

Furniture buying has too many variables and needs too many negotiating skills to be left to a nonprofessional. The alternative of having a hired design consultant order the furniture is not acceptable. The designers may have hidden interests in specifying one system over another. The designers also do not get the same level of discount that a corporation will get, as outlined in the previous section, Think big: The national contract.

Additionally, some design fees will be based on a fixed percentage of the dollar cost of the furniture they specify. Some designers will not charge directly for specifying but may pass on to the corporation less than the full discount they receive.

The facility managers realize that the designer will not do specifications for free. The designer should be compensated on the cost per square foot, as outlined in Chapter 5. The specifications should then go to the furniture buyer for independent verification and processing.

Furniture purchase order process

The furniture purchasing function should be responsible for the acquisition of furniture, carpeting, and furnishings. Furnishings include desk accessories, drapery or window treatment, signage, and general office equipment.

The buyer should be part of the project team. This means that when the designer forwards the design development plans for order purchasing, it is not the first time the buyer has seen the information.

The buyer should have been involved in the process with suggestions on:

- Alternative vendors
- Acceptable and nonacceptable finishes
- National contracts that the corporation may have
- Firms or vendors to avoid for one reason or another
- Ways to prepare the specification for ease of ordering
- Lead times for critical items

The designer's goal is to create a clear, accurate specification that outlines the essential ingredients for an order. The items should be coded to a floor plan so that the vendor can encode which items go to each workstation.

The specification sheet

The essentials of a typical specification sheet listed below include an example for each.

Furniture should be treated as follows:

1. Each item numbered in order to avoid confusion:
   1, 2, 3, or C-1, C-2, D-1, D-2

2. A complete description of the item to be ordered:
   Secretarial posture chair without arms, five arm base with 2¾-inch casters for carpet

3. A separate column for the finishes:
   Base #7211, tan value #2, nylon coat shell #6203

4. A separate column for source:
   Steelcase

5. The manufacturer's catalog number (remember, reversing any two digits will result in a file not a chair!):
   #430-520

   Upholstery is handled in this manner:

1. Source of the upholstery:
   Steelcase

2. Fabric number from manufacturer's catalogue:
   #5261

3. Color choice:
   French Blue

4. Name of the fabric, if any:
   Regis

   Location and quantity are marked up in the following way:

   How many are to be ordered for each workstation?

   12—Room no. 118

   2—Room no. 119B (more than one workstation in room)

   1—Room no. 131

   Costs are determined by the following questions:

1. What is the total required?
   15

2. What is the unit cost after the discount is applied?
   $225

3. What is the extension of the quantity times cost?
   $3375

4. What is the total price including shipping and delivery (if not included in purchase price) plus tax?

Total cost	$3375
Shipping	0 (included in price)
Installation	0 (included in price)
Tax @ 8 percent:	270
Total	$3645

The specification should have this basic project data:

1. Project title, corporation name
2. Building address, floor and related information
3. Project manager's name
4. Date of issuance
5. Design manager or project director's name, telephone number, and street address
6. Each page of the specification numbered as follows:
   _____ of _____ pages
7. A footnote occasionally used to ensure that there *are* foul-ups: Written description supersedes manufacturer's catalog number

The process steps

1. Buyer receives the specification sheets and design development package from the designer via the facility manager. In the case of a minor churn, the request may come from the facility manager without a drawing. An example would be a request to order a chair to match an existing chair.
2. Buyer reviews requests and develops an estimate from vendor's price list or gets one directly by calling the vendor. No commitment is made to vendor at this point.
3. Buyer reviews price with facility manager to ensure that the price is within approved budget or corporate guidelines.
4. Facility manager confirms that expenditure is within approved budget or seeks additional approval. Once the funds are approved, the facility manager authorizes the buyer to proceed.
5. If the item is to be ordered without a bid, it must be classified as within the corporation's minimum bid amount, purchased under a national contract, emergency purchase, matching existing, sole vendor, or unique item.
6. In this case, the item needs to be bid. Buyer will select at least three qualified bidders. Usually a qualified bidder is one that has a widely respected reputation in the industry, has a long-term re-

lationship with corporation, or is known by buyer to have performed well for others.

7. Buyer contacts three vendors to review specifications.
8. Vendors evaluate specifications and submit *sealed* bids by specified date.
9. Buyer has formal bid opening. This is attended by buyer, facility manager, and financial analyst. Buyer records each bid on a bid summary sheet. Each of three reviewers signs each bid on the page containing the total price, and each signs the bid summary sheet. Bid sheet should also be noted with exceptions that distinguish one bid from another: e.g., "does not include delivery," "includes installation," "available in 10 weeks in lieu of 8 weeks."
10. Buyer, because of constant tight schedules, telephones successful bidder with verbal order and purchase order number. If the buyer hasn't called, the bidders will.
11. Buyer issues written purchase order. The typical purchase order contains the same information as on the specification sheet or what was on the vendor's submission for bidding. In some instances, the purchase order may simply state, "See attached specification."
12. The purchase order should have several duplicate copies for both distribution and future use. Suggested color coding for each copy is as follows:
    a. *Original—white.*   Some debate exists on this copy. One school of thought feels that the original should be sent to the vendor. Another school is that the original order should always remain in the buyer's file and the next copy should be forwarded to the vendor. Check with your own corporate auditor and if no one cares, the facility manager/buyer makes the choice. If you are completely automated, why keep any copy?
    b. *File copy—yellow.*   This becomes the buyer's file copy eventually but should remain in the open or active file to ensure follow-up.
    c. *Received Report—green.*   This copy is initially attached to the yellow copy and held in the buyer's file until delivery. At that point, buyer signs green copy as the received report to be forwarded to the financial analyst for logging into asset payables department for payment processing. If the facility manager's area issues its own checks, then the green received report will serve as approval to issue the check.
    d. *Asset Payables—blue.* This copy is forwarded to asset payables or financial analyst to alert of commitment for future payment. Additionally, the monies planned for this purchase

should be deducted from the furniture line in the approved financial document.

 e. Facility manager—pink. This copy is for the facility or project manager's file and for information.

13. Buyer receives order acknowledgement from vendor that reconfirms the pertinent data and, most especially, the delivery date. Buyer compares to original data and reviews any changes with facility manager.

14. About 48 hours prior to delivery, vendor should call to reconfirm delivery. Buyer should have checked the delivery site to ensure that it is ready to receive furniture.

15. Buyer coordinates delivery with facility manager, vendor, building manager (for truck dock and elevators), and construction trades.

16. Buyer receives furniture, oversees delivery, signs for delivery on vendor delivery ticket—which becomes basis for verification of vendor payment—and oversees the installation. An item of furniture may be rejected owing to any damage or because it is a nonconforming piece at this time.

17. Buyer signs green received report.

18. Buyer forwards received report to asset payables for payment.

19. Yellow open file copy is placed in closed file.

20. Buyer updates records for expenditures against the funds allotted for project purchases.

Inventory: Pros and cons

What do the following items have in common? A can of peas and 5000 other items in the grocery store; The New York Times; Playboy *and* Time *magazines; the discarded outer carton from the manufacturer's furniture. The answer is* bar coding.

Inventorying is an awesome task when one does not have the right tools. Now that we have read the answer, let's go back and discover if there is really a question.

Corporations depend upon the facility manager for the completion of the job and for turning over a complete asset to the business manager. If the business manager is to be held responsible for the asset on an individualized basis, an inventory of parts and pieces will be required. If the corporation holds the business manager responsible for the total dollar value of items, then an inventory is not necessarily needed. The facility manager may still want an inventory for future churn work.

The inventory process is relatively simple to figure out: a recorded list of each furniture item and its distinguishing characteristics. In a way, the specification sheet has the information. All one need do is to assign a consecutive number to the item. However, this easy solution becomes a bit more difficult when ordering a workstation that may require anywhere from 10 to 100 components. Each component by itself is useless until combined with the other pieces. Yet if each piece of the workstation is not labeled, what happens when the station is disassembled and moved, and the pieces are distributed to make up two or more other workstations?

What does the facility manager do with this inventory? No sense keeping a typed list since it will be quite long and difficult to manipulate. The answer is to computerize the whole inventory. This entire process takes staff. The buyer would have to log each and every piece into the system, label each piece, and then be certain that every renovation accounted for each component.

If the facility manager already has existing facilities with no inventory tags or systems, then the creation of one is an enormous burden. By the time the rounds are made to tag and inventory the thousands of furniture items, the first items will be moved and reconfigured.

The answer is to rely upon the manufacturers to be resourceful. Let's see if the cartons can be eliminated outright. If each item is shrink-wrapped, the quality control clerk in the manufacturer's factory can verify visually that the right item and color are being shipped.

Additionally, the bar codes that are now on the cartons should be discreetly placed on the components. The manufacturer can figure out where this should be so that is not too visible but can be scanned with a portable bar-coding gun. This still allows the manufacturer to use the information as it currently does for billing and shipping, but it also allows the facility manager, if required, to use the same bar code for inventorying.

While a manufacturer or two may soon offer this, why doesn't Steelcase or Herman Miller provide this as a customer service? The cost should be absorbed in the next price increase. No one likes to pay an extra. Build it in as a marketing expense.

It may be common technology to embed a chip in the component in the near future. This would eliminate any visible bar code complaints (i.e., how come the bar codes don't come in the same finish color?). A scanner could read the chip's information instantly and record it into the computerized system.

The facility manager looks toward the source—the furniture manufacturer—to resolve the issue. As a matter of record, *The New York Times* has a bar code on the newspaper each day. (And they did not ask for my opinion on where to place the bar code.) After shopping at our local supermarket, we get a computerized inventory (shopping list) of everything purchased because each item has a bar code.

Can furniture be far behind?

6.4   The Move-In

A successful facility manager stays that way only by not failing at the eleventh hour. The entire project sequence may take anywhere from 1 month for a minor churn project to 3 or 4 years for a new building. The project is basically over with occupancy of the user.

However, there is one *small* step standing in the way of that success. The facility manager must relocate the staff, the furniture, and 5000 or so boxes from one location to another. The corporation relies on the facility manager to handle this step in stride, without any problems, within budget, and on schedule. What else would be expected of the facility manager? The points below outline the various steps to follow in the flow of the move sequence, some of the terms used by movers, and general methodology.

Moves from one side of the floor to the other, and the relocations involved, and some minor floor-to-floor changes may be handled by in-house porters. The following sequences fit a *major* relocation from an existing facility to another major building, either in the same town or elsewhere. For small moves, the facility manager may delete the steps that are not required.

Move sequence

1. Write a request for proposal (RFP) for professional movers to bid upon. Include scope of move in square feet, number of people, equipment, timing, and location. Write a request to have a move coordinator or move captain designated for each major department or floor to be relocated. The move captains attend all move sequences and participate during the actual move.

2. Select at least three qualified firms to bid. All firms should have experience with major moves, have been in business longer than one can remember, and have a fair number of quality references.

3. Walk through the project with each of the firms so bid price will be as accurate as possible and no surprises will crop up during the move. Be sure to determine whether mover or facility manager will pack contents of individuals and pack shelving items.

4. Receive bids back from firms; evaluate and analyze bids, negotiate final price; award contract to firm with best experience, proper

insurance coverage, best team of movers, and best price. The best is not always the least expensive, nor is it the most expensive.

5. Have designer produce a furniture plan that has names of employees for the new location.

6. Have mover work up a tagging/color-coding system to mark each piece of furniture and equipment that is to move. Mover will mark up the furniture plan, which becomes a move plan.

7. Have mover tag each piece of furniture and equipment.

8. Have mover plot the logistics and sequencing of move with facility manager.

9. Have mover pack, as required, shelving items, and if included, disassemble shelves for relocation and for assembly in the new location.

10. Have mover pack, as required, each individual station or distribute boxes and instructions for employees to use for packing.

11. Arrange, or have mover arrange, for security, truck dock space, elevator time, and special permits that may be required by the local authorities for both the old site and the new site.

12. Have mover hang area numbers that are coordinated with the move plan in new locations. Have move captains check accuracy. Recheck yourself.

13. Commence any premoves, including noncritical equipment, furniture, and contents. Ensure security coverage in new locations while other trades may still be on the site. Make sure walls and floors in both locations are protected. Floors usually get masonite that allows the mover's dollies to move quickly while protecting the floor covering.

14. Oversee installation of new furniture installed prior to general move so that contents can be placed in the workstation without being in the way of the dealer's installation crew.

15. Commence move with move captains present both in old facility to ensure that only properly tagged items are moved and in new locations to ensure that items are delivered to the correct floor and workstation.

16. Have move captains act as your eyes and ears to ensure that all move personnel are working diligently. Have these extra eyes try to tally the number of movers on the job.

17. Take a 15-minute nap, probably 20 hours later, if you get a chance. Get back to work!

18. Arrange for cleaning crew to come in after move (usually a Sunday) and prior to employees' first work day.

19. Have mover or in-house porters on the job all day to remove cartons or other debris when employees unpack. Have move captains prepare any move punchlist items to be given to you.

If all things go according to the facility manager's and mover's plans, then Monday morning will be a day without telephone calls, a day with accolades. You definitely should *not* take this day off to relax. If problems arise, no sense in hiding. Face the situation directly.

Review the punchlist items prepared by the move captains immediately. Assess and evaluate any possible claims against the mover for damages with both the corporation and the mover.

Share your compliments for a successful move with the move team: the move captains and the mover. On major relocations to a multistory building, there probably will be another few weekends more of the same to follow.

No time to rest on your laurels: senior management expects the move to be successful. So get back to the next project or move.

6.5 Postoccupancy Evaluation

After accomplishing the entire move sequence for all floors, assess the real opinion of the staff. This survey of employee reactions to the move, the new space, their new workstations, the colors, and a variety of miscellaneous items is called a postoccupancy evaluation (POE).

The POE, an optional service that is offered by the designer or by independent consultants, is not free, and management may not care to expend any funds on it. The designers have a vested interest in reflecting the success of their plans in making the employees satisfied with their new surroundings. Management will fund a POE when the word-of-mouth rumors of the newly completed space are bad. When management is proud of the space, they may also want a survey in order to "hear" that their investment helped morale. The survey also requires the facility manager's time to coordinate and administer. Finally, management should be prepared to spend money to "correct" employees' perceived issues, if any arise from the POE's analysis.

Ronald Goodrich, the Words of Others author in Chapter 4, is a facilities analyst and environmental psychologist. He developed the sample postoccupancy evaluation form (shown in Tables 6.1 through 6.6 and Figure 6.1) for use by a large corporation after a major upgrade to their building. This information is usually analyzed with a computer. The results are summarized in both written and graphic form for management use. The written report will usually contain recommendations and/or solutions to problems employees may have concerning particular aspects of their new environment.

Postoccupancy evaluation instructions

The questionnaire is divided into six sections.

Section 1 asks for your subjective perceptions of different parts of the physical environment within your own workspace. For each part of the environment there are a series of descriptor pairs. Each pair is separated by seven numbers. For each pair, circle one number which describes best your rating of that particular quality. The numbers closest to the end are the highest rating on either end of the scale. The number 4 is a neutral rating and should be used only when neither descriptor pair adequately describes the physical environment (see Table 6.1).

Section 2 asks for your subjective perceptions of different parts of the surrounding environment beyond your own personal workspace. The same rating system as Section 1 is utilized (see Table 6.2).

Section 3 asks for your opinions about different aspects of the environment. To complete this section, circle one of the five numbers in the scale to the right of the question (see Table 6.3).

Section 4 asks to what extent you are distracted by various events that occur in the office. Additionally, you are asked for your level of satisfaction with several aspects of the corporation (see Table 6.4).

Section 5 is to be used for statistical control and for sorting down our information into meaningful categories. For each question, check, circle, or fill in an appropriate response (see Table 6.5 and Figure 6.1).

Section 6 is optional. This section contains statements about environmental dispositions. Read each statement and think of how it applies to you. Circle the number for each question which indicates how true the statement is for you. This information will be used for research purposes only (see Table 6.6).

If a negative response is received because of failure on your part, you may be facing a postemployment evaluation. However, a successful project should lead to favorable responses on a POE.

6.6   Churn

The World Book Dictionary lists "churn" as a noun with the following definition: "a container or machine in which butter is made from cream by beating or shaking. This causes the tiny globules of fat to come together in pieces that can be gathered as butter;... a violent stirring or shaking."

TABLE 6.1 Yourco, Inc., Postoccupancy Evaluation Section 1: Physical Environment

Personal Work Area

	1	2	3	4	5	6	7	
Standardized	1	2	3	4	5	6	7	Personalized
High-status look	1	2	3	4	5	6	7	Low-status look
Inadequate privacy	1	2	3	4	5	6	7	Adequate privacy
Psychologically comfortable	1	2	3	4	5	6	7	Psychologically uncomfortable
Physically comfortable	1	2	3	4	5	6	7	Physically uncomfortable
Very exposed	1	2	3	4	5	6	7	Very closed in
Noisy	1	2	3	4	5	6	7	Quiet
Cluttered	1	2	3	4	5	6	7	Uncluttered
Well organized	1	2	3	4	5	6	7	Not well organized
Well equipped	1	2	3	4	5	6	7	Not well equipped
Well lit	1	2	3	4	5	6	7	Poorly lit
Better than before move	1	2	3	4	5	6	7	Worse than before move
Like how it feels	1	2	3	4	5	6	7	Dislike how it feels

Work Surface

(desk, table, counter, etc.)	1	2	3	4	5	6	7	
Helps working	1	2	3	4	5	6	7	Hinders working
Well arranged	1	2	3	4	5	6	7	Not well arranged
Adequate	1	2	3	4	5	6	7	Inadequate
Better than before move	1	2	3	4	5	6	7	Worse than before move

Chair

	1	2	3	4	5	6	7	
Comfortable	1	2	3	4	5	6	7	Uncomfortable
Adjustable	1	2	3	4	5	6	7	Unadjustable
Better than before move	1	2	3	4	5	6	7	Worse than before move

Storage

	1	2	3	4	5	6	7	
Adequate	1	2	3	4	5	6	7	Inadequate
Well arranged	1	2	3	4	5	6	7	Not well arranged
Enough for personal items	1	2	3	4	5	6	7	Not enough for personal items
Easy to use	1	2	3	4	5	6	7	Difficult to use
Better than before move	1	2	3	4	5	6	7	Worse than before move

TABLE 6.2   Yourco, Inc., Postoccupancy Evaluation Section 2: Surrounding Environment

General Office Area

	1	2	3	4	5	6	7	
Cold	1	2	3	4	5	6	7	Warm
Orderly	1	2	3	4	5	6	7	Disorderly
Stressful	1	2	3	4	5	6	7	Relaxing
Better than before move	1	2	3	4	5	6	7	Worse than before move
Colorless	1	2	3	4	5	6	7	Colorful
Well designed	1	2	3	4	5	6	7	Not well designed
Well organized	1	2	3	4	5	6	7	Not well organized
Uncluttered	1	2	3	4	5	6	7	Cluttered
Usually active	1	2	3	4	5	6	7	Inactive
Officelike	1	2	3	4	5	6	7	Factorylike
Too little activity	1	2	3	4	5	6	7	Too much activity
Hurts morale	1	2	3	4	5	6	7	Helps morale
Many barriers	1	2	3	4	5	6	7	Few barriers
Machines	1	2	3	4	5	6	7	People
Feels uncrowded	1	2	3	4	5	6	7	Feels crowded
Unattractive	1	2	3	4	5	6	7	Attractive
I like how it feels	1	2	3	4	5	6	7	I dislike how it feels

Lighting

	1	2	3	4	5	6	7	
Helps working	1	2	3	4	5	6	7	Hinders working
Little glare	1	2	3	4	5	6	7	Much glare
Easy to read (print)	1	2	3	4	5	6	7	Difficult to read (print)
Easy to read (VDU)	1	2	3	4	5	6	7	Difficult to read (VDU)
Too little light	1	2	3	4	5	6	7	Too much light
Dislike lighting	1	2	3	4	5	6	7	Like lighting
Worse than before move	1	2	3	4	5	6	7	Better than before move

Noise Level

	1	2	3	4	5	6	7	
Not enough noise	1	2	3	4	5	6	7	Too much noise
Disturbing to me	1	2	3	4	5	6	7	Not disturbing to me
Noise is sporadic	1	2	3	4	5	6	7	Noise is continuous
Machines are noisy	1	2	3	4	5	6	7	Machines are quiet
Noise level is low	1	2	3	4	5	6	7	Noise level is high
Noisier since move	1	2	3	4	5	6	7	Quieter since move
I dislike noise level	1	2	3	4	5	6	7	I like noise level

TABLE 6.3   Yourco, Inc., Postoccupancy Evaluation Section 3: Opinion

	Very little		Some		Very great
To what extent do you feel that you participated in the designing and planning of this space?	1	2	3	4	5
Do you feel that the design and creation of this environment has taken your various personal needs into account?	1	2	3	4	5
Has this new environment lived up to your expectations?	1	2	3	4	5
Upgrading the physical environment means the company is concerned with the feelings and welfare of its employees.	1	2	3	4	5
Have you done something to make your own workplace more comfortable or more your own?	1	2	3	4	5
Does management policy inhibit you from personalizing your workplace?	1	2	3	4	5
Does the environment allow people to learn more about the overall operations of the department?	1	2	3	4	5
Did you have difficulty adapting to the new environment?	1	2	3	4	5
To what extent do you feel different now than you did at first about the environment?	1	2	3	4	5
Do you have enough privacy at your workplace to:					
Do your type of work?	1	2	3	4	5
Communicate privately with others?	1	2	3	4	5
Meet the level of visual privacy that you need?	1	2	3	4	5
Meet your appropriate status in the organization?	1	2	3	4	5
Are you interrupted more frequently since moving?	1	2	3	4	5
Do you have conflicts with others over sharing equipment?	1	2	3	4	5
Can you keep things of value at your workplace without fear of losing them?	1	2	3	4	5
Do you feel you have greater access to your supervisor in the new environment?	1	2	3	4	5

TABLE 6.4   Yourco, Inc., Postoccupancy Evaluation Section 4: Distraction/ Satisfaction Index

How distracted are you by each of the following?	Not at all		Moder- ately	Greatly	
People passing near work area	1	2	3	4	5
People just walking into my personal area	1	2	3	4	5
People stopping to talk to me while passing by	1	2	3	4	5
Visual distractions; something gets my attention	1	2	3	4	5
Certain people who don't lower their voices when talking	1	2	3	4	5
People talking on the telephone	1	2	3	4	5
Noise from telephone or office machine	1	2	3	4	5
I just "feel" the presence of people around me	1	2	3	4	5
Make errors in my work as a result of the distractions	1	2	3	4	5
Take my mind off what I am doing because of distractions	1	2	3	4	5
Usually feel "overloaded"—I hear, see, and am aware of too much going on around me	1	2	3	4	5
How many times a day would you say your work is interrupted by distractions?	1	2	3	4	5

How satisfied are you with each of the following?	Very dis- satisfied		Very satisfied		
Your job	1	2	3	4	5
The people you work with	1	2	3	4	5
The company	1	2	3	4	5
The environment	1	2	3	4	5
Working in this part of town	1	2	3	4	5
Your life in general	1	2	3	4	5
Group morale	1	2	3	4	5

Facility professionals might define "churn" as "the feeling in one's stomach just prior to a major installation or move-in."

Somehow this word that relates to stirring and shaking has come to be defined differently in terms of facilities. The term is probably best defined as "the rate that a corporation's employees or offices are

Sex: ☐ *Male*   ☐ *Female*

Age: ☐ *Under 20*   ☐ *21–30*   ☐ *31–40*   ☐ *41–50*   ☐ *51–60*
☐ *61 and over*

Length of service in company (years):
☐ *Under 1*   ☐ *1–5*   ☐ *6–10*   ☐ *11–15*   ☐ *16–20*
☐ *21 and more*

How many years have you worked in this building?
☐ *Under 1*   ☐ *1–5*   ☐ *6–10*   ☐ *11–15*   ☐ *16–20*
☐ *21 and more*

How long have you worked on this floor?
☐ *under 3 months*   ☐ *3–12 months*   ☐ *over 1 year*

Which accurately describes your position within the company?
☐ *Senior mgmt. (V.P. and above)*   ☐ *Middle mgmt. (A.V.P./manager)*
☐ *First-level mgmt. (Other corp. officer)*   ☐ *Staff (Non-officer)*

Do you consider yourself a part of a work group?
☐ *Yes*   ☐ *No*

How many people do you consider as part of your work group? _____

How many of them can see you sitting at your workspace?   _____

When sitting at your workspace, how many people can you see? _____

How much area do you consider belongs to your personal workspace?
☐ *36 sq. ft. (6 ft × 6 ft)*   ☐ *64 sq ft (8 ft × 8 ft)*
☐ *120 sq ft (10 ft × 12 ft)*   ☐ *More than 120 sq ft*

When seated at your workspace, do you have a view of an outside window?
☐ *No view*   ☐ *Partial view only*   ☐ *Yes, I have a view*

Estimate the distance from your workspace to the window.
☐ *0–8 ft*   ☐ *9–25 ft*   ☐ *25–50 ft*   ☐ *over 50 ft*

Figure 6.1   Yourco Inc., postoccupancy evaluation, Section 5: Statistical information.

moved or renovated." In other words, how often are internal changes made within the corporation?

What is it that turns the facility manager's stomach about a churn project? It is probably the quick turnaround time required to accomplish a significant number of changes in a space that is usually still occupied by employees. This reactive mode doesn't allow the facility manager the normal time to fully plan and administer a well-thought-out facility project. The facility manager is thrown into a situation of

TABLE 6.5   Yourco, Inc., Postoccupancy Evaluation Section 5: Statistical Information, Continued

Describe the boundaries or "walls" of your workspace. On how many sides of your workspace do you have a:	Number of sides				
Full-height wall (floor to ceiling)	0	1	2	3	4
High barrier (cannot see over)	0	1	2	3	4
Medium barrier (can see over when standing)	0	1	2	3	4
Low barrier (can see over when sitting)	0	1	2	3	4
No barrier (no wall, all open)	0	1	2	3	4
Other, please describe _____	0	1	2	3	4

Describe how many times you have participated in each of the changes below since your department has been in its present location	Number of times				
Been relocated to a different space	0	1	2	3	4 +
Rearranged your workspace (yourself or at your request)	0	1	2	3	4 +
Had your job function changed	0	1	2	3	4 +

On an ordinary day, about how many hours (maximum) do you:	Hours per day				
Work alone at your workspace	0	1	2	3	4 +
Work with others at your workspace	0	1	2	3	4 +
Spend time away from your workspace	0	1	2	3	4 +

meeting a predetermined deadline or within the time constraints of a business' marketing plans.

According to the International Facility Management Association's (IFMA) Report No. 1, at least 25 percent of corporations classify themselves with a high churn rate. In this report, a high churn rate means that an average of 60 percent of the employees move within the corporation *each year*.

Another 25 percent reported low churn rates of 10 to 15 percent per year. Therefore, it is assumed that the remaining 50 percent of the corporations move anywhere from 15 to 60 percent of their employees each year.

Why is everyone moving? The facility manager is caught between a rock and a hard place. After all, if the ultimate flexibility is achieved in a corporation, the facility manager is no longer needed!

Do we plan our own obsolescence or our continued employment? Fortunately, the best of the facility managers do plan for as much flexibility as available, but it is still not enough. Some of the principal reasons that cause churn are:

- An increase in staffing due to new business
- An increase in staffing due to increased customer services offered

TABLE 6.6   Yourco, Inc., Postoccupancy evaluation Section 6: Environmental Dispositions

	Very true for me				Not true for me
I hate giving up before I'm absolutely certain I'm licked.	1	2	3	4	5
Sometimes I feel that I shouldn't be working so hard, but something drives me on.	1	2	3	4	5
I thrive on challenging situations; the more challenge I have, the better.	1	2	3	4	5
In comparison with most people I know, I'm very involved in my work.	1	2	3	4	5
It seems as if I need 30 hours a day to finish all the things that I'm faced with.	1	2	3	4	5
In general, I approach my work more seriously than others.	1	2	3	4	5
If I have the choice to be by myself or to be with others, I generally prefer to be by myself.	1	2	3	4	5
Most people that know me would describe me as outgoing.	1	2	3	4	5
I could work in almost any kind of environment. The place that I work in doesn't make any difference to me.	1	2	3	4	5
In general, I need to personalize a space that I work in.	1	2	3	4	5
I believe that hard work makes a better person.	1	2	3	4	5
I believe that a good indication of people's worth is how well they do their job.	1	2	3	4	5
I believe that becoming a success is a matter of hard work. Luck has little or nothing to do with it.	1	2	3	4	5
In general, I find that I am more sensitive to noise and things going on around me than other people seem to be.	1	2	3	4	5
I like to have a place for everything and everything in its place.	1	2	3	4	5
Once I make up my mind, I seldom change it.	1	2	3	4	5

- A decrease in staffing due to a loss of business
- A decrease in staffing due to a cut in service
- A reorganization combining departments
- A change in work flow
- A new business manager reorganizing internally

- A change in business equipment (electronic or mechanical)
- A need to upgrade the image of the area
- A merger with another business

The churn crew is essentially the same group for any other facilities project. The key is to get the team working as fast as possible to expedite the changes. Therefore, the smart facility manager sets up rules and procedures in advance. These rules can simply be a work flow procedure that outlines each responsibility during the change. Chapter 3 contains a generalized listing of these services. However, a specific list of tasks to be accomplished follows. The initial item on the churn procedures list is the most important; it is the transmittal of what is to be done from the end user to the facility manager.

All too often the request for churn is verbal or in a brief memorandum that is not clear. I recommend that the facility manager develop a standard format and insist that it be used. This involves no more red tape than the standard deposit slip, stationery order requisition, or any corporate form. But it *does* organize the end user's vague instructions into concise data.

Have the form printed and distributed as a regular stationery item. This standard request form must include blank space to capture the following information:

Facility services request form

The top half of the form should contain:

- Project title
- Project address, building, floor, zone
- Approximate usable square footage
- Brief description of work to be accomplished, with a space to indicate whether the business wants the actual work to be done or just wants to study the feasibility of making the change
- Date of the request
- Completion dated desired
- Amount of money authorized
- Funding method (capitalized or expensed)
- Name and signature of authorized person who approves the funds (must meet your corporation's signing limitations)

- Name of the user coordinator for daily involvement in accomplishing the churn

The bottom half of the form should have:

- Space to fill in date *actually* received
- Space to fill in name of project or facility manager, with telephone number
- Space to fill in project control number
- Space for facility manager to check off services required to perform the project

The request form should have several copies for the facility manager to distribute after completing the bottom half of the form. Suggested color coding for each copy is shown.

Original—white.   The matter of the fate of the original form is the same as in the discussion for purchase orders in Chapter 6. I recommend that the original stay in your file.

Requestor's Copy—yellow.   Once the form is completed, the facility manager returns this copy to requestor. The requestor keeps a photocopy of the request initially submitted until this copy is received.

Asset payables—blue.   Facility manager forwards this copy to asset payables at the start of the project so that a financial record can be started with the authorized amount as the initial funding. Subsequent changes in the project may require that additional funds be approved. These approvals get forwarded to asset payables as necessary.

Other copies.   Additional different copies may be required to alert specific units of work depending on size and scope of the corporation's facilities department. For example, in very large departments, a form may be sent to each of the following units: architectural/interior design, engineering, construction, and furniture purchasing.

Churn work flow procedures

Listed below are procedures with responsibilities to be performed during the life cycle of a churn. The key personnel usually associated with the task are highlighted after each step. The key used is as follows:

Facility manager, project or construction manager

Designer or architect

Engineer

Buyer of furniture, furnishings, and equipment

User coordinator or contact

The procedures and the personnel involved are these:

- User funnels request for change through coordinator and sends to facility manager.
  U F

- Request form is verified and completed.
  F

- Request form is distributed.
  F D E B U

- Meeting is held to commence project.
  F D E U

- Feasibility study, drawings are prepared, approved by user.
  F D E U

- Drawings are issued for estimates.
  F B

- Estimates are received, reviewed, and approved.
  F U

- Construction work is accomplished, furniture ordered and installed.
  F D E B U

- Punchlist is completed, financial closing of project.
  F D E B U

Warehousing.   These steps can take a few days on a small project or as long as several months on a major churn project. Section 5.3 outlines how to save time by hiring external consultants by using an annual on-call agreement with fees predetermined and negotiated. Another time-saving idea may be through the use of stock on hand for furniture and carpet. This enables the facility manager to fulfill some of the furniture and carpeting needs from a readily available surplus. This can save months in a churn project's life cycle.

Carpet.   Carpet tile, as a widely accepted practice, is usually ordered with a moderate amount of extra tiles. The amount ordered beyond the actual need should vary with the size of the order. A small project may require the facility manager to purchase up to 10 percent extra.

But larger jobs may need only 3 to 5 percent extra. The extra tile cost should be built into the initial project cost.

In addition to replacing damaged or lost tiles, the extra tiles become a surplus stock that matches the existing dye lot. This surplus becomes instantly available to accommodate modest additions to a department or replacement tile for pieces damaged during the renovation.

If the facility manager has a national contract with a vendor, a stocking program may be successfully negotiated into the contract deal. In other cases, storage space should be planned for by the facility manager.

Furniture.   Furniture is more difficult to handle as surplus for several reasons:

- Items take up far more space than carpet tiles.

- Neatly boxed tiles are stacked easily, while the furniture comes in different shapes and is easily damaged if stacked.

- Moving furniture to and from a warehouse requires major trucking efforts.

- Justifying purchasing 10 percent extra furniture to sit in a warehouse for possible future use is difficult.

Therefore, the furniture warehouse ends up as a depository of unused, unwanted surplus items, but it can be a manageable item with some preplanning.

Try to use an existing corporate warehouse if this idea is appealing. Otherwise, extra funding is required to lease space. The cost for relocating surplus to or from the warehouse is a direct charge to the user with the furniture. The mover who performs the relocation can be contracted for negotiated pricing for warehouse moves.

Every item that is sent to or from the warehouse must be inventoried. (Where is that bar code?). No sense in accumulating 20,000 square feet of items and not knowing what they are. This whole procedure requires people. The resources may be internal or external, with proper security. There is a price to be paid for the ease of future churn. The end may justify the means. The facility manager can accommodate modest changes, requests for a few odd pieces, and instant needs.

The alternative—negotiating a stocking program with the manufacturer or using their quick-ship programs—has advantages. The quick-ship or rapid-response-type programs have limited sizes, colors, and finishes readily available. Some items ship as early as 1 week and as late as 4 weeks. This is probably as fast as the facility manager can take it since some construction changes usually have to be made first.

The manufacturer can also stock items, but if they are produced specifically for your corporation, the facility manager's approval may be required for payment in advance of installation. A restocking program planned between the manufacturer and the facility manager may be a more acceptable solution. The facility manager and the manufacturer work together to estimate the corporation's minimal needs on a regular basis. This can be based on past orders or anticipated volume. When the facility manager draws down the stock below the minimum level, the manufacturer will automatically refill the order.

The manufacturer program means that all furniture will always be new and at a negotiated cost. Reused stock from the warehouse is significantly lower in final cost. The hidden cost, as outlined above, is in rental expense, personnel costs, refinishing costs, and moving expenses.

I analyzed 5 years of utilizing surplus furniture versus purchasing all new. The cumulative impact appears to be a net saving of about 25 percent per year for an ongoing operation. This is probably enough to justify a warehouse procedure if the start-up expenses can be funded.

The purchase order process steps outlined in the previous section would be amended. The additional step would have the buyer review available stock in the warehouse for use on the project in lieu of ordering new. The saves of reusing existing versus the cost of new should be maintained to justify the program over the first few years.

Furnishings.   Other restocking programs can be negotiated with vendors if your corporation has a standards programs. An example is desk accessories. If your standard program includes stock manufacturer items for pens, calendars, etc., then the vendor can utilize the same type of restocking program defined above. The best of all worlds for the facility manager is to have the vendor stock standard items at no charge with an agreement to purchase, within reason, the average number of items per year. This way accessories are available and paid for by the facility manager or buyer when needed.

The facility manager has several alternative solutions available to reduce the stress caused by churn. Careful planning, proper selling to management, and a rational, logical approach during the time of irrational behavior by the end user should be the facility manager's course.

Perhaps the facility manager can alter the dictionary definition of "churn" from "to shake or agitate with violence or continued motion" to one that reflects how the smart facility managers define it: "change from one state to another through continued motion."

6.7   The Words of Others—National Contracts

Robert C. Pew   *Chairman and Chief Executive Officer, Steelcase, Inc., The Office Environment Company*

The author is right. National contracts offer many benefits to the facility manager. But national contracts are more than legal arrangements, more than a means to the best possible price for the customer. They are, in fact, expressions of trust, indications of a commitment to a mutually profitable long-term relationship between customers, dealers, designers, and manufacturers.

The real value of a national contract often lies beyond the quality of product and its capability as a functional tool. The customer should always evaluate the services the manufacturer has to offer. Often, these services are the keys to cost-containment measures that will benefit the facility manager for years after the contract is signed.

What are these services? Facility managers should look to manufacturers to provide such services as:

- Computer-aided support programs that streamline and simplify the order entry/inventory process
- Access to in-depth office environment and ergonomic research and development findings
- Customer involvement in new product development
- Reputation for on-time delivery and expedited shipment programs
- Educational programs that support or supplement in-house facility manager activities
- International services that assure high, consistent quality worldwide
- Manufacturing capabilities to meet quality and quantity requirements
- A commitment to its distribution system (dealer organization)

The last point is particularly important because the dealer is the most effective interface between the supplier and the user. No manufacturer can provide on-site assistance as well as a trained, committed, professional local representative. And no dealer can be all those things without a solid commitment from the supplier he or she represents.

The art (science?) of facilities management is new, emerging, changing on an almost daily basis. The days when the purchasing agent chose suppliers simply on the basis of price and delivery are virtually gone.

Today, when facility managers are looking for the single "one-stop shopping" source, they must look at potential suppliers almost as partners in the business of facilities management.

First-cost considerations are important. But life-cycle costs provide a truer profile of a supplier's effectiveness. And one way to assure yourself of the lowest possible life-cycle cost is to choose a supplier that provides ongoing nonproduct support.

Construction Management Approach

7.1 Introduction

Corporations rely upon in-house facility managers for overall control of projects. The initial feasibility phase through the furniture purchasing phase accounts for only 50 percent of the churn project expenditures. On new building projects, these same expenditures may account for only 30 percent of the costs. The remaining costs are basically attributed to construction.

Once the corporation has embraced facilities management, the concept of adding construction management is a natural extension. In small corporations, the role of the construction manager may also be performed by the facility manager. In large corporations, this role is performed by another person.

The alternative of no construction management within the corporation is not acceptable. The reasons are similar to those for having facility management. The construction management role is essential to ensure that the project:

- Gets built in accordance with plans and specifications
- Stays within approved budgets
- Stays on schedule
- Adheres to corporate standards and guidelines
- Adheres to applicable local, state, and federal regulations
- Adheres to Yourco standards
- Gets filed with local regulatory agencies
- Has acceptable construction techniques and practices performed on the construction site

The role that is occasionally confused with the construction manager's is that of general contractor. The general contractor (GC) is responsible for hiring the various trades, for managing these trades, and for overall relationship with the workers. On small churn projects, the construction manager can also double as the general contractor. On larger projects, the construction manager will not have sufficient time to perform both roles. Additionally, the GC will normally be an external firm on the larger projects.

Since construction accounts for approximately one-half of the time and dollars, senior management might raise a few questions. Why haven't:

- Project responsibilities shifted to construction managers?
- Construction managers tried to take over the process?
- Facility managers had to fight to retain this leadership?

The answer is *politics*.

Every corporation has a method of handling situations, people, and conflicts. The political pressure of contacts, carefully worded statements, and "pecking order" are items to be contended with by facility and construction managers.

A construction manager's role is mainly with the GC and trades in the field. The contact with the corporation is basically limited to project meetings. It is probably safe to estimate that 37 of 40 hours in a workweek are conducted by the construction manager without contact with the users. This is by plan, not by chance. You are the principal liaison with the user.

This means you are responsible for all political negotiations, constant communications (in-person and telephone), and overall budget control. The facility manager is always *on*. Construction managers seem to have limited interest in the other aspects of the project. Facility managers seem determined to retain the full project responsibilities. This has resulted in the project management structure.

The successful facility manager recognizes that project management is a team effort. A productive team wins the game every time. Facility managers need not flaunt their leadership. Smart facility managers make the most of their talented resources and don't abuse them.

7.2 Construction Management Function on the Job

Chapter 3 briefly outlined the responsibilities of the construction manager. This section covers the specific activities the construction manager performs during the project.

The construction manager has been participating in project meetings as a member of the project team. The first action is to arrive at cost estimates early in the project to secure preliminary expenditure forecasts.

Cost estimates

A construction manager receives a partially completed drawing (or a substantially incomplete drawing) of architectural and engineering plans. The construction manager obtains the best and most reliable prices on the basis of this sketchy information. It is always interesting to note that corporations requiring cost estimates at this stage of the project believe the costs are "gospel."

The estimated construction numbers are as good as possible. The later the estimates are required, the more architectural and engineering details will have been drawn. This leads to more accurate estimates. When estimates are required early in the project, construction and facility managers work closely together to analyze several factors affecting the price.

Image. The level of finish of goods and materials will vary greatly with the image of the department. An example is wall covering:

- Executive areas may get upgraded wood panels.
- Customer contact areas may get silk wallpaper.
- General office areas may get vinyl wall covering.
- Operational areas may get painted walls.

The same price variation is true for ordering standard versus custom-made pieces. The higher the image, generally, the higher the cost.

Timing. There are three views of a project's completion:

- User: optimistic, expects an early finish
- Construction manager: pessimistic, forecasts a late finish
- Facility manager: realistic, quotes Murphy's law (What can go wrong will go wrong). However, you will be as realistic as possible and forecast a date between the two.

To finish early, the construction manager may require overtime expenditures or may order an off-the-shelf item, which conflicts with the original specifications.

Bidding. The most competitive price is assured if the construction manager has an opportunity to prepare a request for proposal (RFP).

This allows the construction manager to prequalify three or more bidders. The qualifications would include a proven record of quality workmanship and successful project completions.

Cost per square foot.   At this point in the project the only way to give a price, without a definitive drawing, is with the cost per square foot method. The construction manager may utilize historical knowledge and recent project costs actually spent to arrive at a "dollars per square foot" estimate. This unit price is multiplied by the usable square footage to be built to arrive at the estimated construction cost.

If there is no construction manager or there is a lack of historical data, you can get assistance from one or more of the following external sources:

- Construction general contractors
- Direct input from subcontractors
- Companies that specialize in estimating only and are not tied into any contractor to guarantee the facility manager an accurate forecast
- Various literature that offers current data: *F. W. Dodge Report*, *Buildings* Magazine, *R. S. Means Report*, Building Owners and Managers Association (BOMA), U.S. Department of Commerce, U.S. Department of Labor

After the construction costs are estimated, there are additional costs to cover the general contractor's fee and general conditions. These costs are at a fixed percentage and subject to negotiation. Each is calculated separately on the total of all trades and not on top of each other.

Fees

The fee represents the GC's profit on the project and ranges from 5 to 8 percent. This percentage is highly negotiable and subject to many variables, including:

- Size of the project
- Length of relationship between GC and owner
- Skills of the facility/construction manager
- Project location
- Project complexity

General conditions

This represents costs incurred by the GC for various project overhead expenses. This percentage may vary from 8 to 15 percent. The general conditions are subject to negotiations based on scope and complexity of the work. The percentage is reduced by what is provided by the construction and facility managers from the items required to manage the construction process. The general conditions include:

Field office. Rent, purchase, utilities, alterations

Equipment. Major machinery, small tools and supplies, automobile and trucking expenses

Site conditions. Temporary buildings, ramps, roads, fire protection, scaffolding, hoists, snow removal, elevators, temporary heat, light, power, water, and toilets

General cleaning. Housekeeping, dirt chutes, rubbish removal, glass cleaning

General expenses. Office equipment, blueprints, mock-ups, surveys, safety, communications, test and inspection services

Personnel. Supervision and staff, fringe benefits, taxes

Insurance. Workman's compensation, liability, bonds, builder's risk coverage

Request for proposal

This is also referred to as request for quotation (RFQ). The request for proposal (RFP) is sent to prequalified bidders to supply detailed cost estimates based on a written outline of work to be performed, and normally a complete set of contract documents. Contract documents are all drawings and specifications necessary for project construction, including:

Architectural and interior design plans

Demolition plan. Items to be removed in an interior churn project, including lighting, partitions, electrical and telephone outlets

Partition plan. Exact location of new partitions to be erected and the type of partition required

Reflected ceiling plan. Exact location of each ceiling item, including light fixtures and air-handling grilles; specifications of each item included

Telephone and electric plan. Exact location of each outlet and any special circuitry or wiring required

Architectural plan.   Special cabinetry or other special items

Furniture plan.   Layout of furniture and equipment

Equipment plan.   Schedule of all equipment referenced by coding to furniture plan. Equipment attributes on this plan are: power and telecommunications requirements; cabling lengths, restrictions, specifications; and physical characteristics: size, weight, egress, and heat output.

Engineering plans

HVAC plan.   Sheet metal, grilles, vents, and other items to provide heating, ventilation, and air-conditioning

Plumbing plan.   Plumbing requirements for bathrooms, kitchen, chilled water

Electrical plan.   Circuitry, panel, and other items to supply sufficient power to meet requirements

Sprinkler plan.   Exact layout of each sprinkler head and piping layout, and sprinkler head specification

Safety and fire plan.   Fire-suppression system, smoke detectors, fire extinguishers, and appropriate signage for exiting

Security plan.   Required devices and equipment for securing the floor(s) and the building, including closed-circuit television cameras and monitors, access systems, alarm locations

Cabling plan.   Layout of local area network, trading floor cabling, etc.

Structural plan.   Additional steel, concrete, or other items that must be added to support a change in the building's basic structure

Bidding.   Bids are returned sealed. Bids are opened and signed by the construction manager, the facility manager, and the financial analyst. The process ends with an award of the contract.

Construction phase

Progress.   Construction managers monitor project progress to guarantee adherence to plans, schedule, and budgets. Construction manager remains in constant contact with GC in case of any slippage. When there is a variation from the plan, schedule, or budget, the construction manager and the GC resolve the situation in the best and least expensive manner.

Requisitions.   GC submits monthly requisitions for payment. Construction managers determine if invoiced work is actually completed. Normal construction practice is to retain 10 percent of approved amount as retainage. Retainer account is held by construction manager until the project is closed out. At that point, the balance is forwarded to the GC as the final payment. Requisitions include breakdown of actual time and materials used or ordered in the month. There is *no* premium paid on work performed early in the project. Such attempts for extra funds are a ploy by the GC to use your corporation's funds at the start of the work.

Cost reports. The construction manager and financial analyst maintain complete data on all invoices as compared with original budget, original bid, costs to date, and anticipated cost to complete. This report is updated each month and supplied to you for inclusion in the project's overall reporting.

Installations. Construction managers oversee the completion of all work, equipment, and systems. The construction work and the punchlist should be completed prior to the user's move-in.

Postoccupancy phase

- *Guarantees and warranties.* All mechanical and electrical systems should be tested and checked out under full load conditions. Necessary maintenance contracts should be placed in action. The basic equipment is turned over to the user. Guarantees for structure, waterproofing, roofing, etc., should be obtained and turned over to the user. If the equipment is within your building, then the building office would receive these guarantees and warranties.

- *Building start-up.* New buildings require that a procedure be written to run the building's equipment properly. This should include training of staff in system operations.

- *Operations.* Construction managers should prepare or have prepared documentation manuals for equipment (make, model, serial number, manufacturer, maintenance schedule, function, location) and systems (life safety, light, power, HVAC, security, fire protection).

- *Financial closing.* GC submits a final requisition at construction's end. Construction managers' responsibilities include confirming that:
  - All obligations of GC have been covered in terms of base contract and/or any change orders.
  - Punchlist is accepted and signed off by facility manager.
  - Systems have been tested.
  - Guarantees, warranties have been turned over.
  - Final payment has been issued to contractor.

- Liens have been released, signifying that contractor has received balance of money due, including the retainer. (This lien waiver should cover all other construction vendors and subcontractors. Construction manager may have the GC supply separate lien releases from each subcontractor.)
- Final project financial summary has been prepared to reflect final expenditures as compared with original forecasts and bids

The teamwork approach should result in a minimal amount of conflict between the facility manager and the construction manager.

7.3 Construction Documentation

As reviewed in the last section, there is a significant amount of documentation required throughout the construction phase of the project. This section outlines basic contracts that the facility manager and construction manager use. These are only highlights of clauses; exact wording varies within each corporation. Always have a qualified person (lawyer) review the contracts.

TWO-PARTY AGREEMENT
BETWEEN CORPORATION AS GC AND SUBCONTRACTORS

This agreement is by and between Yourco (OWNER) and the Subcontractor (SUB) dated (month) (day), (year).

AGREEMENT

SUB agrees to furnish and pay for all materials, labor, tools, equipment, permits, taxes, hoisting its own materials, and everything that is necessary for the proper completion of construction (WORK) described below and in accordance with:

- contract documents supplied by architect/interior designer (name of person or firm)
- general conditions
- insurance coverage required

SCOPE

OWNER and SUB agree that the work to be done and the labor and materials to be supplied are called WORK and are described as follows:

_____

_____

PRICE

The contract price for the above WORK to be paid to SUB by OWNER is $ _____ , subject to any additions and/or deductions that may be approved by OWNER.

INVOICES

SUB shall submit on or about the first of each month a written requisition for payment due for all WORK that was performed for the month past. The requisition will reflect actual WORK done or a percentage of WORK if appropriate less a 10 percent retainage.

Invoice will also reflect the following information:

- total value of contract
- payments made to date by OWNER
- payments made by OWNER to others on behalf of SUB
- anticipated amount left to complete contract
- percentage of WORK completed
- OWNER will pay net amount due, excluding retainer

OTHER TERMS

OWNER's lawyers will surely want to add several other clauses.

INSURANCE (SUGGESTED AMOUNTS SUBJECT TO ACTUAL WORK)

- Worker's compensation as required by statute
    - including employer's liability limit of $100,000
- Comprehensive General Liability
    - each occurrence, bodily injury, $2,000,000
    - each occurrence, property damage, $500,000
- Comprehensive Automobile Liability
    - each occurrence, bodily injury, $1,000,000
    - each person, bodily injury, $500,000
    - each occurrence, property damage, $500,000

APPROVALS

_____	_____
(Name of OWNER official)	(Name of SUB official)
_____	_____
(Signature)	(Signature)
_____	_____
(Date)	(Date)

TWO-PARTY AGREEMENT
BETWEEN CORPORATION AND GENERAL CONTRACTOR

The highlights below are from a standard form of contract.

AGREEMENT

This contract is dated (month) (day), (year), by and between Yourco (OWNER) having its principal office at _____ and the General Contractor (GC) having its principal office at _____ .

GC shall provide and furnish all labor, materials, appliances, appurtenances, supplies, and services of every kind and nature for the com-

plete performance of all the WORK herein described_____
in the State of _____ in accordance with the plans, specifications, drawings, details and information (PLANS) prepared by ARCHITECT.

OWNER shall pay GC for the full and complete performance of this contract, subject to additions and deductions the sum of $.

GC OBLIGATIONS

GC shall furnish all materials, fixtures, equipment, labor, and supervision necessary for the prosecution and completion of the WORK.

OWNER'S OBLIGATIONS FOR PAYMENT

GC shall submit to OWNER on the _____ day of each month a written requisition with same information as outlined in the invoice section above.

POSSIBLE INCREASE IN COSTS OF CONTRACTOR

GC and OWNER agree they are aware of the possibility of increases in the price of labor and materials. GC shall make *no* claim for an increase in the Contract Price. It is understood that any and all risks of increase in price of labor and materials have been contemplated by GC and have been taken into full consideration in arriving at the Contract Price.

TIME

Time is of the essence in this Contract. GC will proceed in a prompt and diligent manner. If GC does not protest within five days after receipt of a schedule change as to its unreasonableness, such failure to protest shall be deemed acceptance of the schedule.

PERFORMANCE OF THE WORK

WORK shall be completed by _____ .

WORK TO OWNER'S SATISFACTION

OWNER may notify GC within five days of any work that is deemed unsatisfactory. WORK will be repaired or corrected, or an adjustment made in the price from the value of WORK as it should have been performed versus value as actually performed.

INSPECTION

GC shall provide at the site, at all times, sufficient, safe, and proper facilities for the inspection of the WORK by the OWNER.

DAMAGES AND DELAYS

Either side may claim a delay or damage due to the other's interference within two days of occurrence.

DEFECTIVE WORK OF OTHERS

GC agrees that the proper, workmanlike, and accurate performance of the WORK depends on other contractors and subcontractors performing in a workmanlike manner.

PLANS AND SHOP DRAWINGS

GC confirms that the plans are sufficient for their intended purposes and that the WORK can be successfully performed and completed in accordance therewith.

SUPERVISION

GC shall furnish a competent representative constantly on the site to receive notices, orders, and instructions.

UNLOADING AND STORAGE OF MATERIALS

GC shall unload, receive, sort, properly protect, and store all materials to be set under this contract, furnished by others as delivered to the site.

SAMPLES OF MATERIALS

GC shall furnish samples of materials to be used and they shall be identical with materials actually used.

WORK OF OTHER TRADES

GC will repair any damage done by itself or by subcontractors.

SAFETY

GC will use best efforts to prevent accidents to workers and shall comply with all laws, regulations, and codes concerning safety applicable to the work and to safety standards established during the work by OWNER.

PROTECTION TO ADJACENT PROPERTY

GC shall maintain adequate protection for the owners of adjacent property from injuries or damage arising from the carrying out of this Contract.

CLEAN-UP

GC shall remove and clear any dirt or debris caused by the execution of this work.

TAXES

GC shall pay all social security, other taxes and contributions imposed upon it as an employer and furnish evidence to OWNER of payment, when so requested.

TERMINATION

Any breach by GC of Contract term; then OWNER shall have the right, after a grace period, to supply workers, materials, etc., for the completion of WORK. The costs, including legal fees, shall be charged to the GC.

INSURANCE

- Workmen's Compensation and Employer's Liability Insurance
- Public Liability Insurance
- Theft and Extended Coverage Insurance

- Insurance covering adjacent property
- Automobile Liability Insurance

ASSIGNMENTS AND SUBLETTING

GC may not sublet any work without OWNER approval.

LIENS

GC shall deliver work free of any and all liens, claims, chattel mortgages, and conditional sales agreements of third parties.

GC WARRANTIES

GC shall furnish to OWNER written certificate covering all work and all warranties and guarantees of subcontractors, manufacturers of appliances. All such warranties shall run for a period of one year or longer from the later of:

- building completed and accepted by OWNER
- date of permanent certificate of occupancy

LABOR PROVISIONS

GC will not employ workers or means that may cause labor disturbances or stoppage.

ARBITRATION

Only dispute to be arbitrated is the cost of Changes. Such dispute to be settled by arbitration in the County of _____ pursuant to Construction Industry Arbitration Rules of the American Arbitration Association.

DISPUTES

Except for arbitration, shall be in the venue of the County of _____ .

PATENTS

GC agrees to indemnify and hold harmless OWNER from loss or damage due to any infringement.

PERMITS AND COMPLIANCE WITH RULES AND REGULATIONS

GC's sole responsibility is to arrange for all tests, inspections, permits, licenses, and fees required for the proper prosecution and completion of the WORK.

ADVERTISING/SIGNS

GC shall not place any sign whatsoever without the written approval of OWNER. GC shall not advertise any work from OWNER without prior written approval of OWNER.

CONFIDENTIALITY

GC shall not divulge to third parties without written consent of OWNER any confidential information obtained in the course of performing the Contract.

ETHICAL STANDARDS

GC shall not make or offer any benefit upon anyone to influence the conduct of such person (NO BRIBES).

SECURITY

GC shall at all times from the beginning to the completion of the WORK, including nights, Saturdays, Sundays, and holidays, provide all necessary and proper safeguards in and around the WORK to the OWNER's satisfaction.

NOTICES

All notices to be in writing, deemed to be given if sent registered or certified mail, return receipt requested, addressed to:

For OWNER: Name and address of corporate facility/construction manager

For GC: Name and address of GC

ENTIRE AGREEMENT

This contract covers all agreements between the parties.

APPLICABLE LAW

This agreement is governed by the laws of the State of _____ .

APPROVALS

For OWNER: _____

(Signature, title, date)

For GC: _____

(Signature, title, date)

Standard forms

All standard forms should be signed, dated, and witnessed.

WAIVER OF LIEN

That (Contractor) _____ existing by virtue of the laws of the State _____ and having an office at _____ for and in consideration of payment received by the Contractor pursuant to a certain Contract dated _____ by and between Contractor and (Owner) _____ which Contract provides for the performance of certain Work and/or supplying of certain materials in connection with the construction of a (Project) _____ at a total cost of $ _____ of which the Contractor has been paid $_____ and of which the amount retained has been $_____ pursuant to the Contract for labor performed and materials previously furnished.

Contractor does hereby, for itself/successors and assigns, forever release and waive the right to file any notice of lien pursuant to the Lien Law of the State of _____ on account of any labor performed and/or materials furnished prior to the date hereof, whether pursuant to the Contract or otherwise in connection with the Contract.

CONTRACTOR'S STATEMENT

The (Contractor) _____

certifies to (Owner) _____

with reference to Contract dated _____

in connection with construction a (Project) _____

that Contractor has received as of this date $_____ the balance, excluding retainers, due is $_____ and is sufficient to complete Contractor's obligations.

Undersigned knows no reason why Work will not be completed in accordance with terms and conditions of the Contract.

The following constitutes a complete list of all subs:

Subcontractor/Supplier	Amount Due	Amount Paid
1. _____	_____	_____
2. _____	_____	_____
3. _____	_____	_____

Final payment waiver of lien.   This is the same as waiver of lien except that contractor acknowledges payment in full for any and all such labor and/or materials so furnished for the project.

Contractor's warranty certificate.   In addition to contractor and owner addresses and names:

- Contractor certifies that all materials and equipment furnished under the contract were new unless otherwise specified.
- Contractor will promptly correct all work rejected by owner that fails to conform to contract.
- State length of warranty. See Warranties, above.

Equal employment opportunity (EEO) provisions.   Contractor makes a statement complying with all applicable laws regarding EEO that contractor will not discriminate against any employee or applicant because of race, creed, color, sex, or national origin.

Summary

The firm, warm handclasp as a bond of work to be done is still preferred. Unfortunately, in this highly technical and exacting world, it is necessary to reduce all basic commitments to writing. A contract does not set up an adverse relationship. In fact, the contract is the basis for a mutual understanding of each of the party's roles and responsibilities. With a good team, many of the clauses may never be utilized.

7.4 The Words of Others—Construction Management Approach

Jerome Paul   *Vice President, The Lema Organization, Inc.*

The Construction Management approach has gained great acceptance in the building industry in the past 10 years for some very good reasons.

Although the author has outlined the fundamentals, I would like to share with you some of my thoughts on the subject. My experience centers primarily on interior renovation and/or new interior construction projects that fall within a dollar range of $250,000 to $10,000,000.

Generally in projects of this nature, the construction manager also fills the role of general contractor. Why has this approach gained such popularity? To understand this, one must understand the shortcomings of the traditional approach that is becoming worn with time. This approach can result in a disaster.

The traditional approach of an owner:

- Using in-house facilities management department
- Coupled with consultants (architect and engineer)
- To bid out a project
- On a lump-sum basis
- To three or more prequalified general contractors
- Usually to satisfy a corporate competitive bidding requirement

I am always reminded of the astronaut riding to the moon on a vehicle built by thousands of "low bidders." It can be a dangerous voyage.

Most facility managers operate on the belief that through this practice they will receive the best cost estimates for their company. My observations of the estimating practices of some general contractors lead me to believe that a good deal of estimating is a "game of numbers." Because the general contractor (GC) is "under the competitive gun," the GC must come up with the "low number."

To achieve this, the GC may produce a bid that can only be done after a great deal of "buying out." The GC more often than not will achieve a profit or fee on a lump-sum project by "squeezing" the sub-contractors on their prices. Sometimes this is accomplished by using subcontractors that are best described as marginal as to their performance—but their prices are low! No matter how hard a GC tries to perform on a project, the GC is totally dependent on the subcontractors.

A low bidder and a close second low bidder may be low for all the wrong reasons, including omissions which sooner or later will be apparent to the owner or facility manager. We in the construction field are all too familiar with projects that become nightmares, ending up at an arbitration table.

How can this be avoided?

One method, if properly understood by all parties to a project, is the construction management approach. The most important task a facility manager has in undertaking this approach is to choose the "right" construction manager for the job.

Some GCs try to sell themselves as construction managers but can never "let go" of the GC mentality. They see the construction management approach as a "ploy" to negotiate work with a client.

I have heard of a construction manager (and I use the term loosely) using a "controller" or "salesperson" to act as project manager on rather involved projects. You can imagine the result of such practices. A facility manager should insist on meeting with the construction manager's staff and should carefully review their credentials. Make sure your proposed project manager has a track record and will not be using your job to gain experience.

Assuming that the facility manager has made the right choice of a construction manager, some other important factors should be recognized. No matter how professional a construction manager may be, we are all human and cannot perform the impossible.

Two important ingredients to success are realistic time frames and realistic budgets. Usually in the type of projects I have been involved with, the construction manager's input during the "preconstruction" phase is a minimum as to both budgeting and job schedules. These are usually presented to the construction manager by the facility manager.

The time frame of a project from my experience is usually presented to the facility manager by an operating department head and has nothing to do with the realities of good construction practices. Unfortunately, this occurrence is all too frequent and results in uneconomical project costs where "overtime" and "excessive spending" are used to make the time frame.

However, there are some projects that start on the right footing, with the construction manager chosen early enough to assist the facility manager and the project consultants in establishing both a realistic project budget (ideally with some contingency money) and a project time that is achievable and realistic.

The competitive bidding requirement is usually met since the construction manager will bid competitively, assuming there is enough time, close to 90 percent of the cost ingredients of a project. The remaining costs are general conditions and the construction management fee, which has clearly been established early on.

It is important to carefully preselect the subcontractors and review a suspicious low bid to establish a good team of subcontractors. The financial character of the subcontractor should also be subject to investigation.

Ideally, the construction management approach is a team approach with the old adversarial nature of the lump-sum contract discarded. The construction manager knows the fee in advance and is assured of a profit on a project.

The quality of the construction manager's performance, if high, usually can ensure future projects, and that should be enough incentive to perform and to make a project successful.

Third Stage:
Applying the Basics
to the Fourth Dimension
of Time

Chapter

8

The "Dumb" Facility/"Smart" Facility Manager

8.1 Introduction

Planning building interiors encompasses several distinct challenges for the corporate facility manager. These challenges include dealing with a stock of existing office buildings that are not "smart" but instead are filled with inadequacies and chronic shortfalls.

The facility manager has to deal with the realities of the office working environment, with available furniture systems and with well-educated office workers.

Your first challenge is the initial installation where the following elements need to be balanced:

- "Hundreds" of different tools must be utilized by many different business units within one building structure. Can this building accommodate the planned occupants?

- Businesses have specific locational requirements. Is this building in the right place? Can the various departments stack correctly into this building's configuration?

- Workers are the key to the business. Can they be placed logically, efficiently, effectively within their business units and within their workplace?

Your second challenge is the never-ending story of corporate *churn*. Churn—the reconfiguration of office facilities to accommodate business change—creates new demands on you:

- You must have the ability to accommodate new technology, as well as new power and air-conditioning demands.

- There is a need to improve wire management and increase the worker's effectiveness through the furniture systems.

- An ability is required to make work flow changes based on electronic capabilities in lieu of the physical flow of paper in a straight-line pattern.

- Well-educated employees are aware of building ills. When an employee mentions TBS, it is not Turner Broadcasting System, but Tight Building Syndrome.

- There is a constant awareness of toxicity. New building sites must have environmental studies for toxic or other potentially hazardous materials. Leasing space in older buildings requires environmental analysis for contaminants such as asbestos (found as a spray-on fireproofing material) and formaldehyde (found in office furnishings and building insulating materials).

- There are changes in the business' nature. What they're doing and how they do it has changed.

Your third challenge can best be appreciated by those working in a large corporation already—*politics*. You face politics throughout the project life cycle:

- What is the relationship of the new building site to the residence of the seniormost manager moving to the site?

- In what floor will senior management be located?

- What floor am "I" on? How far am "I" to senior management?

- What image are you planning for "my" customer-contact business unit? "We" must project the proper ambiance and level of finish to customers (ourselves, our peers, our recruits, our leaders).

- What's "my" view?

- Do "I" get my own bathroom?

- How many corner offices on a floor? Which one is mine?

With these three challenges in mind, you are ready to face the "dumb" facility as it relates to:

- The realities of the working environment
- Balanced capabilities of management
- The missed opportunities
- Chronic shortfalls

- Furniture systems
- The office as an employee benefit

This chapter explores differences between the facility manager who has certain beliefs and myths that are held sacred, and the "smart" facility manager.

8.2   Realities of the Working Environment

When planning building interiors, the facility manager must be able to accommodate the three basic components of the working environment: Tools, Place, Workers.

Listed for each component is the commonly accepted belief and the reality of what the facility manager faces. Keep in mind that these views are from a perspective of the space within a corporation with massive changes. Facility managers within small companies face the same or similar problems on a lesser scale.

Belief	Reality
Tools	
Today's automation equipment will be the same when the move is made.	Automation equipment serves the current function and may not be useful within a year. The business manager continually needs tools that are faster, smarter, and cheaper.
Communications equipment will be "smarter" at the time of the move and will be adaptable.	Communications equipment is often what's available, not necessarily what's needed or affordable. When relocating to an existing building, businesses may have to accept existing telecommunications systems in lieu of what is actually required.
All furniture systems accommodate planned corporate technology.	Furniture components should be able to accommodate technology for the fourth dimension of *time*. However, furniture manufacturers await computer vendors' release of equipment size and shape. Many furniture speciality components are based on 2- to 3-year-old computer technology.
Microsystems are flexible and change with the business.	Microsystems are out of date either by design or through rapid business change. Systems that adapt live on—but not on their own accord. They live on because very busy software consultants are constantly in demand to write new programs for aging systems.

Belief	Reality
Place	
Management wants buildings to be located where safety, shelter, and business are equally balanced.	Final site is subject to the best price, proximity to customers, and the senior manager's residence.
Management requires maximum employee comfort in new buildings or renovated facilities.	Planned comfort and amenities are fleeting. They are sacrificed to accommodate business expansion.
Management feels that the building's infrastructure can accommodate all tools.	"Dumb" old buildings just cannot accommodate office technology tools, especially if excessive wiring, electrical power needs, and air-conditioning are mandatory.
Management wants to provide for fun and pleasure in the building.	Maybe a fitness center or an atrium works into the building. The average worker should be in the office from 9 a.m. to 12 noon and 1 p.m. to 5 p.m. This leaves very little time for fun in the office. Atria may provide employees with a diversion, but fun is questionable.
Workers	
The business plan drives all other criteria.	All too often the facility or space plan drives the business.
Management feels that workers should be up to date in their knowledge of business purposes.	Workers and managers come and go. Business knowledge is fleeting. The mysterious business plan is just beyond your grasp. With the rate of corporate mobility, the business plan tends to be so personalized by the current manager that the next manager may not agree with its principles.
A trained employee remembers forever.	Once trained is not enough. Refresher courses are absolutely necessary. You should retrain staff on use of basic office equipment. Why spend extra for flexible, movable components if the staff does not know how to change them?
Workers are motivated through knowledge, training, and attractive facilities.	Workers expect all of the above, and they need the three Ps: pat on the back, promotion/push up the corporate ladder, and pay raise.
Management feels that employee satisfaction is shown by their accomplishments and within their workplace.	Satisfaction is individualized and very personal.
Workers expect that a certain amount of daily socialization is automatically tolerated by management.	Socializing may be encouraged by management attitude and through furniture orientation.

Belief	Reality
Workers	
Employees should have a say in the layout of their workstations.	Workstation should be designed for the current function, not the current worker.
Employees can decorate their space.	Yes, but within the confines of the workstation. An open plan office should have no penetration above the panel height (nominally 62–68 inches).
The worker can work in any space and condition.	Workers want more space, recognition, and air.
Business managers always consider workers and facility managers when compiling business plans or next year's budget.	An attitudinal shift is required for business managers to invite you to participate in goal setting and in business planning. Employees participate in setting their individual goals.

Balanced capabilities

Realities of planning for the building interiors vary considerably from beliefs. You must seek a method to bring this difference into balance. The following are some points to keep in mind:

- Tools, place, and people in harmony works as an ideal goal, but you have two ingredients to contend with: money and "keeping up with the Joneses."

- Get more for more of your resources up front; you will not necessarily get another chance. Spending more initially for staff needs can be justified by productivity gains. It doesn't matter if the unit is a line operation or a profit center.

- Imbalance from planned growth is workable.

- Unplanned imbalance from unplanned growth is why the corporation has such a high churn or renovation rate.

- Facility managers can encourage vendors to retrain the worker in the use of furniture and equipment.

- Local business managers can arrange periodic refresher courses in tools used by the worker.

- Tools enhance the employees; they don't replace them.

- Facility managers can never overcome management jealousy. It strives on differences in office size, location, and level of finish. Smart facility managers learn to tolerate it from the managers.

- Overcome building inadequacies by planning on corrective measures over a sustained period when immediate funding is not available. Plan on raised flooring, new risers, and better heating, ventilation, and air-conditioning systems.

The missed opportunities

The following table shows some common myths and the missed opportunities these myths represent:

Myth	Missed opportunity
Everyone moves a lot.	Although a corporation may have a 25 percent churn rate, not everybody is moved in a 4-year cycle. Identify the mobile unit(s) and plan accordingly.
Everyone loves the open office.	Modified open planning is the way of life. After all, 10 percent of the staff who have enclosed offices (senior management) approves the open plan for the other 90 percent (staff).
Fun isn't work.	Create an interesting building. It attracts the business or corporate clients and keeps them as tenants.
The place of the office doesn't matter.	Back to jealousy—status is everything. A manager's salary is not known, but office size and location are well known.
People can adapt.	Staff do not adapt; they accept and remember.
Money talks: the more you spend, the better.	Corporations look at all expenses and incomes—the bottom line.
Managers say, "If I can't see 'em, they're not working."	Encourage productivity through planning, effective work flows, and good layout and design. Research tells us that visual supervision does *not* ensure they're working.

Chronic shortfalls

There are a number of areas in which chronic shortfalls are common. For each, there is a list of items of concern followed by some comments about these concerns.

Buildings

Lighting quality

Quantity of electrical power

Cooling capacities

Power, communications distribution infrastructure

Control of heating, ventilation, and air-conditioning

Vertical transportation, elevatoring for multifloor users, alternatives for movement of people and equipment

Open area acoustics

Management attitudes about place

Builders address their new buildings in terms of how the building will be constructed. In the future, let's seek out how the building will be used. Smart business managers realize that using dollar cost and location are not the only criteria for judging buildings. Builders' concern for future usage of buildings should eliminate or reduce standard shortfalls.

Furniture and technology

Wire management

Acoustics

Visual noise

Microsystems application

Cramped clerical space—once technology is installed

Furniture manufacturers continue to struggle with the "right" way to go. A few years ago, devices were introduced that cranked up, down, left, and right. Manufacturers followed the devices by increasing the height of raceways at panel bases from 4 to 7 inches. Recently, manufacturers added raceways at the top and the middle of panels (at desk height).

Tools

Clumsy, awkward interconnections

Inconsistent ergonomics

Dimensional incompatibility

Environmental sensitivity

Demands of vendors for service accessibility

Non-user-friendly tools

Unfortunately, your battle to accommodate wider, deeper, higher, and heavier tools than furniture systems can handle continues. The logistics are unbelievable to wire large amphenols through standard grommets.

Workers

Training workers on "officing"

Management attitude

Sense of control and participation by workers

Environmental understanding

Only 10 percent of staff participate in layout, design, and color selection. Increase staff involvement—arrange presentations and previews of planned changes. Accept suggestions subject to final review.

Furniture systems

Some facts about first- and second-generation furniture systems are listed below; they are followed by some wishes for third-generation systems.

First generation
    Panels with hang-on work surfaces and plastic files
    Heavy, difficult to move assemblies
    Too tall (80 inches)
    Limited colors and fabrics
    Technological solutions that were required but nonexistent
    Limited componentry

Second generation
    Wire management solutions
    Ergonomic workstations and seating
    Nearly unlimited design manipulation of furniture
    Systems integration of environmental issues
    Accommodation of microsystems with minimal problems
    Availability of all heights
    Virtually unlimited fabrics and colors
    Nearly unlimited systems flexibility

Third generation
    Ability to connect same manufacturer's different systems
    Ability to connect different manufacturers' systems
    Option on use of panels to support furniture
    Standard and special items delivered within 8 weeks
    Unlimited flexibility and interchangeability
    Unlimited colors, fabrics, and finishes

Unlimited personalization with no extra expense
Wrist rests on articulated keyboards
Easier assembly and disassembly
Opportunity to fine-tune worker's microenvironment: air-conditioning, heating, lighting

The office as an employee benefit

This phrase was first coined by Mike Tatum, the Words of Others author in this chapter. Considerable management time is expended on employee financial benefits. The benefits of the office are often overlooked. Listed in the table below are some comparisons.

Criterion	Typical benefit	Office environment
Purpose	Enhances allegiance and productivity	Enhances effectiveness and allegiance
Costs	Extremely high and usually unquestioned	Differential less than other benefits
Usage	Must leave work to use all benefits	Can use all day, every day on the job
Value	Indirect and comparative	Direct and comparative
Visibility	Invisible and intangible	Visible all day, every day, and tangible

Summary

A 1985 study stated that the manager asked to coordinate an office move deserves hazardous duty pay. Not because the relocation tasks can be nerve-frazzling, which they can, but because of the likely impact on the manager's career.

The study found that 68 percent of managers responsible for arranging corporate moves were either *demoted* or *fired* after the move because of foul-ups during the move, or reduced job performance resulting from the stressful experience.

On the other hand, in 1988 facility managers are far more educated and trained to handle the shortfalls and other situations covered in this chapter. Builders will provide you with smart buildings. You will guarantee that staff are better wired, more comfortable, and more productive through built-ins, including smarter and cheaper:

- Telecommunications systems, including teleconferencing, networking, and telephone systems
- Wire (fiber-optics) and wireless technologies (radio transmission)

- Energy and building management systems

- Access flooring for maximum flexibility and instant accessibility to wiring.

Your future is brightened by the fact that total flexibility will soon be achievable and within the worker's individual control. Today's smart facility managers embrace technology and avoid tomorrow's dumb problems.

8.3 On Being a "Smart" Facility Manager

Being called "smart" is an interesting term. The actual definition, courtesy of The World Book Dictionary, *is: "quick at learning; clever and bright; sharp and shrewd in dealing with others."*

Technology used to deliver your corporate products is still growing and increasing in sophistication. The November/December 1987 issue of *Facilities Design and Management Magazine* listed 80 different manufacturers of prewired panels. Each listing was classified into the following attributes: five criteria of power distribution, four criteria of power capacity, four criteria of cable capacity, and four criteria of power access.

There is probably no way for you to memorize every attribute for every manufacturer. Of course, you're familiar with your own systems. However, you must keep current with the industry.

The previous section discussed ways that buildings can be "smart" through designs that are more responsive to user needs. Smart buildings can easily accommodate new technology. But not every corporate business needs high-tech connections. Not yet.

How do you get "smart" or remain "smart"? The answer is through education. There are several ways to get or maintain your own personal education:

- Educational seminars

- Reading

- Listening

- Doing

- Associations

Educational seminars

Numerous courses are available through universities. Most facilities managers receive announcements by being on the mailing list of a trade magazine. If funding is a problem this year, request the money for next year. Keep trying until it's approved. These courses are usually taught by fellow professionals interested in furthering the education of others.

There are hundreds of conferences and seminars given at the regional and national level. The list below, courtesy of *Facilities Design and Management Magazine,* reflects the variety of seminars available to you in a typical year. And this is only a partial listing of conferences.

- A E C Exposition
  Show and conference for architects and engineers
- American Society of Interior Designers (ASID)
  Conference
- American Institute of Architects (AIA)
  National conference
- Building Owners and Managers Association (BOMA)
  Show and conference
- Business of Design
  Institute of Business Designers (IBD) annual conference
- Canadian Facility Management
  Show and conference
- DesCon/Facilities
  Annual conference, International Facilities Management Association
- Designer's Saturday and International Design Center of New York Fall Markets
  Features Facilities Management Day
- Designers' Market Southwest
  American Society of Interior Designers (ASID)
- Government Workplace (General Services Administration)
  Seminars, trade show
- International Facility Management Association (IFMA)
  Annual conference and exhibition
- Lighting World: International Advanced Illumination Exposition and Conference
  International Association of Lighting Designers, Illuminating Engineering Society of North America, Southern California Section of Illuminating Engineering Society
- National Association of Corporate Realtors (NACORE)
  Conference and exhibition

- National University Teleconference Network
  Annual conference
- NEOCON, World Congress of Environmental Planning and Design
  Features Facilities Management Day
- North American Telecommunications Association (NATA)
  National convention
- Pan Pacific Lighting Show
- Society of Industrial and Office Realtors
  Conference
- South West Facilities Conference
  Arizona chapter, IFMA
- Westweek, Pacific Design Center
  Conference and exhibition
- Workspace
  Annual conference

Reading

Facilities managers should be reading trade magazines. Articles cover up-to-date techniques and products being used. Advertisements and "new products" features also display the latest. Chapter 9 reviews the trade magazines.

Additional literature is always available through the reader response card at the back of the magazine. This gets you current information and a follow-up call from the vendor.

Several catalogs are available. About the best and most comprehensive is Sweet's Catalog. There are about 16 volumes to a set. You must first qualify to receive the set, and there is a mailing charge.

Read this book, again.

Listening

Always pay attention at project meetings, vendor interviews, and seminars. Among the nonessential things overheard, there are occasionally new and valuable bits of information. I have not stopped listening and learning. I attend monthly International Facility Management Association chapter meetings where a different facility concern is discussed each session by an expert in that discipline. In 5 years of meetings, I don't believe a single topic has been repeated. But, eventually it will, because technology has moved to the next level of sophistication.

Doing

The idea of having firsthand knowledge is appropriate. No better way to learn than to experience and try out products, techniques, and innovations for yourself. Most corporations cannot afford for you to make mistakes.

Be careful. An example: a new furniture system may be tested by churning a small, 10-workstation project. Certainly, consider this before buying 750 workstations of an untested product for that headquarters project.

If you don't have the opportunity—or funding—to try a product, firm, or technique, seek out someone who has. These contacts can be made through IFMA or through the vendor. The vendor should *not* be with you when you go through your colleague's facility.

Associations—AIA, ASID, BOMA, IBD, IFMA, NACORE, NATA, et al.

All organizations and associations listed above, and others, are excellent in serving the facility professional. In my opinion, the best *overall* is the International Facility Management Association.

I have been with IFMA since 1982, when the association was 2 years old. The goals of this book and IFMA are about the same:

- Support the field of facility management with education and research, and provide up-to-date information.

- Create an awareness of facility management's value within the corporation.

- Develop and maintain high standards of ethics.

If you are not a member, I recommend joining. If you are a member, you already know the benefits. Stay a member. This is not an exclusive club. Every association member listed above belongs in IFMA.

Dual membership is a necessity. Keep current in your own discipline with your association membership. Keep current with the profession through membership in IFMA.

8.4   The Words of Others—Smart Facilities and Dumb Environments

Michael D. Tatum   *Principal,*
Michael D. Tatum Consulting

"Smart" facilities can be developed in (many) "dumb" buildings. "Dumb" environments can be developed in (all) "smart" buildings.

Perhaps some definitions are in order. If we simply define "smart" as "information-rich" and "dumb" as "information-starved," it will suffice for now. Fine. So how do those definitions fit environments, facilities, buildings?

Most "facilities" aren't

Environments may be "dumb" or "smart"—that is, based upon information-starved processes and decisions or based upon information-rich processes and decisions. Facilities are environments which truly facilitate the full range of purposes of their occupancy, and they can *only* do so if based upon information-rich processes and decisions. So facilities are, by definition, "smart" (and *only* "smart") environments.

Dumb buildings.   Buildings (that is, building "shells and cores," ready to receive working environments) may be either "dumb" or "smart." But here, current semantic abuse rushes in to confuse the issue. A "dumb" building is a simple enough concept—a building based upon information-starved processes and decisions, as most speculative office buildings are. Most real estate investors, developers, brokers, and shell-and-core architects have little direct experience in planning, designing, engineering, constructing, maintaining, and managing the myriad details of a broad range of their tenants' everyday interior working environments. They lack critical information upon which to base their decisions and actions. And even the best "generic tenant" information may miss specific needs of any particular tenant. Such is the nonspecific nature of speculative office building development.

Smart buildings?   Now to the phenomenon and often spurious definition of "smart buildings." Smart buildings, as commonly referred to, focus information-rich processes of design upon communications and computer systems built into them to provide an array of telecommunications, computing, security, HVAC and lighting control, and other shared tenant services. Such buildings may or may not be "smart" (that is, based upon information-rich processes and decisions) in a multitude of other ways, such as those which affect effective floor layout, replanning flexibility, privacy, and acoustics, et cetera. Many "smart buildings" are examples of unbalanced intelligence, the architectural equivalent of the "computer nerd" who processes very deep knowledge in a single area but is disfunctional in many major aspects of everyday life.

Dumb buildings can be changed....   Dumb buildings can become the homes of smart facilities so long as the building can learn the new information—that is, so long as the building can be reasonably modified to become supportive of unanticipated needs at a feasible cost. In various circumstances you may have to make such basic changes as:

- Adding (many tons) of HVAC chiller capacity
- Retrofitting entire floors with elevated floor systems
- Replacing entire suspended ceilings: grid, board, and lighting
- Reinforcing many bays of structure
- Doubling or tripling electrical power at floor panels
- Adding stairways for exit requirements
- Reglazing all windows for energy conservation, comfort, leakage
- Retrofitting sprinklers and other life safety elements
- As well as the increasingly common problem of asbestos abatement or encapsulation.

...Unless they have disabilities.   But you may discover buildings (hopefully, before it's too late) with disabilities which are beyond your capacity to reasonably change. This could include such problems as:

- Inability to achieve effective floor layouts because of quirky (curved, angular, notched) floorplate shapes; inconsistent glass to core depths; difficult column placements; strange locations or angles of core elements; scattered core access points, etc.
- Inability to achieve equal amounts of windows in offices of equal size to avoid status wars
- Inability to achieve perimeter zone comfort or energy efficiency in a nonreflective, single-glazed, poorly insulated curtain wall

Note that many of the above problems could occur in buildings which might be called "smart buildings" by previous (as well as by popular) definition. Some problems of common usage permeate virtually all rental office space—"smart," "dumb," or otherwise. For example, though over half our office space is open plan nationally, the "building standard" acoustical ceiling in more than 95 percent of rental office buildings is mineral fiber board, at its best seriously inadequate for open plan noise reduction. How "smart" could those buildings (and their open plan occupants) be?

Dumb environmental development processes.   The vast majority of my career has been and, alas, still is spent participating in dumb environmental development processes. They are the rule rather than the exception. Though they are survivable, sometimes even with amazingly high-quality results, the results are in spite of, not because of, the dumb process. The dumb process is represented by characteristics such as:

- "Bass ackward" priorities.   In which the appropriate holistic priorities such as occupant effectiveness and occupant satisfaction become secondary to priorities such as:
    - "Cram 'em in."
    - "We didn't plan ahead so time's the top priority."
    - "Never mind their creative individuality, give 'em hyperstandardized workstations.

- *Fragmented, conflicting, parochial responsibilities.*   Which pit each contributing group's most narrow, self-serving attitudes against the holistic priorities. This sometimes seems like a contest to sink any potential for the forthcoming environment's being a true "facility." No one is rewarded for the holistic viewpoint.

- *Vast resources devoted to CYA (cover your asterisk) documentation.*   At great cost and almost no productive yield to the process. This fetish for heavily documented studies, analyses, justifications takes tremendous percentages of a project's total time, budgets, and effort—and it takes that time and money away from the potential of meeting the holistic goals.

- *Safe, risk-free, progress-free approaches.*   By many team members whose seeming motto is "if it ain't broadly recognized as broke, I'm certainly not going to be the one to even surface the possibility that improvement is possible." At the best, in this viewpoint, a change (even a certain improvement) simply means more work for the already overworked.

- *Cost-centered thinking.*   Which views working environments as having no "bottom line upside," that is, little or no potential to positively affect productivity or the operating bottom line of the organization. *Except*—Yesterday's conventional wisdom as embodied in this viewpoint sees that the *only* positive way for facilities to have an impact on the balance sheet is by cutting their costs (and resultantly reducing occupant effectiveness).

If the above looks familiar, you're really beginning to understand the real worlds of "facilities" development and "facilities" management. I place "facilities" in quotation marks because, in most cases, working environments don't "facilitate" the mission of their occupants very well. And the process described above facilitates ulcers more than it does effective environment.

So why do we do it?

Because we are making progress, and because, as remarked the circus roustabouts following the elephants with a shovel and a wheelbarrow, "It's show business!"

Smart facilities development processes. "Okay, you've told us about dumb environmental development processes. So what are smart processes like and how do we get there?" Nag, nag, nag. You're always looking for solutions, and simple, quick solutions at that. All right, here it is.

Holistic priorities. Adopt priorities like occupant effectiveness and occupant proficiency as your personal responsibilities. Never mind that you're not rewarded for this.

Holistic team responsibilities. Convince top management that *all* contributors to the facilities development process should adopt the holistic goals, be responsible for them, and be rewarded for meeting them.

Trusting team environments. Now that everyone's working toward the same holistic goals and is rewarded for the same nonconflicting accomplishments, this should be easy. Then you can devote all the CYA energy, time, and money to the real tasks. That alone should put you over the top.

Stay constantly at risk. By always advocating changes that will improve the potential of facilities to meet organizational goals. Do it even in the face of the crusty CEO who says, "I don't give a damn what some egghead in Research says about productivity. Git those panels low enough so I can see the b _____ s *work!*"

Understand and advocate your organization's mission. Devote yourself to a clear, "global" view of the organization, its priorities and culture, the changes in both short- and long-term directions. Insist that your executive leadership share the essential information with you. They'll understand the importance of facilities in the long-term strategies for which they've made clear plans. Won't they?

Cost-to-benefit ratio thinking. Is clearly the new way you will all consider facilities development. You'll use your research-based as well as your practice-based knowledge to constantly evaluate probable costs against probable benefits of the particular element. The benefit side of the facility ledger will be constantly evaluated and promoted.

So there you are. Just six things to do. Simple, straightforward, understandable. They may not be the complete answer, but they're close enough for corporate work. It'll probably take a couple of weeks, maybe even months for you to get 'em done. But they'll make a world of difference. Honest.

Perceptions of a Marketed Facility Manager

9.1 Introduction

A facility manager acts as a problem solver, pyschologist, business manager, negotiator, environmentalist, economist, engineer, space planner, buyer, designer, political activist, and baby-sitter. And we tend to enjoy our corporate role.

With the heavy work load of a facility manager, why bother to single out the marketing staffs of external consultants? Why bother to highlight the marketing staffs' strong and weak points?

Time spent now results in time saved for you in the future. Remember, this section deals with the fourth dimension of time. After reading this, the following wonderful events will occur:

- All those great marketing agents and representatives will *change* their techniques.

- Your tools will improve, and you will be more careful in your review of consultants.

- Marketing representatives will have a better understanding of their target market.

- Marketing representatives' pitches will be to the point and fact-filled.

Prior to outlining the various marketing techniques, it is interesting to note who is the target market. Besides the facility manager, marketing staffs pitch their firm to design and architectural staff members, furniture buyers, construction managers, senior management, and *the* senior manager, the chief executive officer. Of course, there is cross-selling. The furniture market staffs also sell to external architectural and design firms.

Interestingly enough, you also market to some of the same in-house people. While the facility manager may be saying, "Sorry, I don't have a project or purchase at this time," it is possible for the senior manager to be rejecting your request for funding.

An accurate, to the point presentation that takes a minimal amount of time is probably the most successful method to achieve closure for *all* of us.

Rather than continually refer to our marketing friends as agents, representatives, or staffs, I'll use a term that I fondly call them: "marketeers" (in memory of the Mickey Mouse Club).

The marketeers are an amazing group. They are totally dedicated to their current firms. And when they change jobs, they are totally dedicated to their new firms. They always speak well of their former position, but "my new firm is better because..." Marketeers are a necessary part of the business. How else would you know which facility manager is doing what with whom? Where would the trade magazines get all those great 8 × 10-inch glossy color photographs?

Many college students take *Principles of Marketing*. The course book for "Marketing 101" lists the essential methods utilized to market a firm's talents.

- Trade shows
- Publicity/trade magazines
- Direct mail/testimonials
- Brochures
- Cold canvas calls
- In-person presentations

Surprisingly, "Marketing 101" is one of only a handful of liberal arts classes with "real-life" applications. (When is the last time you needed social studies?) This section follows the use and abuse of those marketing techniques.

9.2 How *Not* to Market the Facility Manager

At every conference trade show, vendor booths are filled with marketeers. Every third letter received in the office is from a marketeer. Every trade magazine contains one or more articles carefully photographed and placed by marketeers. And you could have two meals a day for 6 months without seeing the same marketeer twice. Herein lie the views of facility managers who have been *marketeered out*.

Trade shows

Firms take a 100-square-foot trade show booth with the expectation that more than 1000 facility managers will stop. Getting a small percentage of you to stop justifies the booth.

Normally, the booth is filled with photographs of the firm's best projects. Yet the photos show only space, unoccupied by people! What do you see when you stop?

Stairways	Angled, curved, and straight
Conference rooms	Board, customer, and meeting rooms
Reception areas	Modern, traditional, and minimalist
Exterior shots	Entrances, parking lots, and sunsets behind the building
Corridors	Skylit, carpeted, and with sconces
Cafeterias	Scatter, single-line, and neon-lit

It would be great if there were photos of space actually occupied by people. With the exception of one person in the reception area, none of the above spaces are used by staff for work—none show workstations.

Can this firm do any layout and design? Why not post some blueprints to show the planning ability? Has this firm done any open planning? Firms tend to overlook the fact that the facility manager is seeking firms that can design and draft. Let the facility managers see some details.

Can the person staffing the booth answer questions intelligently? Nothing is more frustrating than the booth attendant's not really understanding the questions posed by the facility manager.

Publicity/trade magazines

Several trade magazines feature articles on recently completed projects. The marketeers are very talented. They have already analyzed their particular target and articles appear in strategic magazines. These articles can appear from various viewpoints with the right magazine selection. Listed below for each viewpoint are the most appropriate magazines the marketeer would select.

Facility manager
Facilities Design & Management

Architect
Architectural Record

Architecture

Progressive Architecture

Senior manager
Corporate Design

Designer
Interior Design

Design Graphics World

Professional Office Design

Furniture buyer
Contract

Floor Covering Weekly

Realtor
Real Estate Forum

Realty

The New York Times: Sunday real estate section

Engineer
Architectural & Engineering Systems

Engineering News Record

Office manager
Modern Office Technology

Constructor/owner
Builder

Buildings

Buildings Design Journal

Constructor

Professional Builder

Unfortunately, the same trade show photos are used in these magazines and periodicals. More stairways, corridors, and exterior shots are seen. At least the photographs are accompanied by an article with some information. While there is a definite need to reflect a firm's design and decorative abilities, this is too much.

Facility managers should get any trade magazine that offers a complimentary subscription. This is an inexpensive way to keep up with the profession and your colleagues. The magazines have different views of the same topic.

If you feel a magazine does not serve a purpose, drop the subscription. The magazines are eager to add (or retain) your name on their subscription list because it helps their advertisers. On the other hand, the magazines with sustained readership are a clue to what other facility managers consider to be the quality magazines.

Here is a synopsis of what you read in a typical issue. Selected for this review are magazines received by me in September 1987.

Facilities Design & Management

- Subtitle: For Corporate Executives, Managers, and Planners of Office Environments
- Publishes 10 issues per year
- Published by Gralla Publications, New York
- Copublishers: Janet L. Ryan, Anne Fallucchi
- Editor: Anne Fallucchi
- Circulated free of charge to qualified individuals actively engaged in office facilities planning and design for their corporations
- All other U.S. subscriptions $55 per year
- Regular features
  - Letters to editor
  - Editorial
  - Facilities news
  - Association news
  - Real estate news
  - Telecommunications news
  - Upcoming calendar of events
  - Current literature
  - Classified ads
  - Index of advertisers
- September 1987 issue features
  - Hughes Aircraft's move to new Los Angeles headquarters, interview with president, photo montage, list of credits to facilities team
  - CIGNA's PC-based system for project management tracking, including detailed flow chart of the system's structure
  - Source guide to CAFM software in 41 applications
  - Preview of the Designer's Saturday and IDCNY Fall Market (New York City's NEOCON), including all facility seminars on Facilities Thursday and product offerings
- Remarks
  - This is probably the best overall magazine covering the facility management profession.

- Articles are not manufacturer-oriented. The photos are good, but there are not enough interior shots.
- News sections are up to date and cover salient items.
- It runs about 134 pages.
- This periodical is a definite must for the facility manager.

Architectural Record
- Combined with *American Architect* and *Western Architect and Engineer*
- Subtitle: Business Design Engineering
- Publishes 14 issues per year
- Published by McGraw-Hill, Inc., New York
- Publisher: Ted R. Meredith
- Editor: Mildred F. Schmertz
- Subscription rates for personnel of architectural, engineering, interior design, design, and other directly related firms and students thereof: United States and U.S. possessions: $35
- Regular features
  - Letters
  - Editorial
  - Business news
  - Design news
  - Literature
  - Calendar
  - Classified ads
  - Advertisers index
- September 1987 issue features
  - Construction economy update based on Dodge Reports
  - Study of school architecture
  - Review of Vollum Institute for Advanced Biomedical Research
  - Review of new museum and research complex for the Smithsonian Institution
- Remarks
  - This contains excellent, detailed architectural coverage.
  - There are also informative line drawings and floor plans.
  - Alas, there are 105 full-page ads out of 196 pages in this issue.

Architecture
- Incorporating *Architectural Technology*
- Subtitle: The official magazine of The American Institute of Architects

- Publishes 12 issues per year
- Published by the American Institute of Architects
- Publisher: Bob Kliesch
- Editor in chief: Donald Canty
- Subscription rate is $35 per year in the United States, and the publisher reserves the right to refuse unqualified subscriptions
- Regular features
  - Letters
  - News
  - Events
  - Literature
  - Advertisers
  - Technical tips
- September 1987 issue features
  - World architecture, 14 countries surveyed through photographs and line drawings
  - Global look at construction
  - Space frames, outer and inner space
  - Roofing that responds to specific climatic conditions
  - Marketing lessons from abroad
- Remarks
  - This is a good architectural magazine with photos of buildings and grounds.
  - There is not a single shot of any office interior.
  - The issue runs about 150 pages
  - This is for architects, only.

Corporate Design

- Subtitle: The magazine for the facilities/interiors planning team
- Publishes six issues per year
- Published by Cahners Publishing Company
- Publisher: Daniel E. Comiskey
- Editor: Philip G. Schreiner
- Free for the asking, no rates or qualifications shown
- Regular features
  - Editorial
  - New products
  - Databank
  - Advertisers
  - No letters accepted

- September/October 1987 issue features
  - Alabama Power headquarters with photos, commentary, and credits for project team
  - Boring Smith headquarters with photos, etc.
  - Robert Martin Co. headquarters
  - Asbury Park Press headquarters
  - Deloitte Haskins & Sells Princeton offices
  - A Kansas City law firm's headquarters
  - MCI Southeast Region headquarters
- Remarks
  - This magazine has had a few name changes in the past 2 years.
  - In search of an identity, it seems to have settled on half as many issues and corporate headquarters.
  - It runs 120 pages.
  - This magazine has seen better days, and we look forward to its return. Publication was suspended in January 1988.

Professional Office Design

- Publishes six issues per year
- Published by the New York Law Publishing Company
- Copublishers: Clinton W. Alphen and Steven A. Farbman
- Editor: Muriel R. Chess
- Regular features
  - Editorial
  - Design news
  - Products
  - Arts and antiques
  - Advertisers
  - No letters
- September/October 1987 issue features
  - Office of the future, thoughts by architects and designers
  - Lighting: balancing office brightness
  - Short history of Computer Support furniture (all ads)
  - The role of the construction manager (good article)
  - Four articles on installations submitted by designer, all crediting the designer and the products without any mention that a facility manager was on the team
- Remarks
  - This is a glossy set of disguised advertisements for architects and interior designers, and products they selected on a particular project.

- An occasional good article is sandwiched between the photos of reception rooms and stairways.
- There are only 81 pages to flip through.
- The magazine is making efforts.

Design Graphics World

- Publishes 12 issues per year
- Published by Communication Channels, Inc.
- Publisher: Gregory Herring
- Editor: James J. Maivald
- Free subscription to qualified professionals; annual subscription $24 for United States, including Hawaii and Puerto Rico
- Regular features
  - Calendar
  - Classifieds
  - Industry news and newsmakers
  - Literature
  - The marketplace
  - Products, including hardware and a buyer's guide
- October 1987 issue features
  - Micros and Workstations: Price vs. power
  - Video Imaging: Window to a new world
  - Hardware vs. Software: Has software bridged the capability gap?
  - Combine CAD and models for teamwork that pays
- Remarks
  - This one is highly specialized in computer-aided product news.
  - If you are into electronic graphics, then you should be receiving this magazine.
  - With only 66 pages, you are through it before your second sip of coffee.

Contract

- Subtitle: The Business Magazine of Commercial Furnishings, Interior Design, & Architecture
- Publishes 12 issues per year
- Published by Gralla Publications
- Copublishers: Len Corlin and Gary S. Puro
- Editor: Len Corlin
- Subscription price $20 for 1 year for firms and individuals who specify, design, buy, or replace contract furnishings; all other U.S. subscriptions $55 per year

- Regular features
  - Editorial
  - Letters
  - Contract news
  - Cartoon of the month
  - Product features
  - People news
  - Calendar
  - Literature
  - Classifieds
  - Advertisers
- September 1987 issue features
  - Designer's Saturday update, including the facilities management schedule
  - Bank & Dramatic Building Find Harmony
    Branches are essential for customers, but they represent less than 20 percent of a financial institution's space. Yet, when reading this annual tribute to banks, you would think that everyone works in a branch.
  - Two additional highlight articles on other branch bank designs
- Remarks
  - This is one of the better magazines for contract personnel.
  - Again, if you are into contract work, read it.
  - The 210 pages contain ads from about 110 different advertisers.

Buildings

- Subtitle: The Facilities Construction and Management Magazine
- Publishes 12 issues per year
- Published by Stamats Communications, Inc.
- Publisher: Ray J. Walther
- Editor: Craig A. Henrich
- Complimentary subscription to professionals; others pay $45 per year in the United States, its possessions, Canada
- Regular features
  - Editorial
  - Projections
  - News and ideas
  - Classifieds
  - Calendar
  - Ad index
- September 1987 issue features
  - Top 120 corporate real estate departments

- Top 400 development and/or management firms statistics and data on volume and usage
- Top 90 government agencies/universities—The Government of Canada is number one with 320 million square feet.
- Remarks
  - This is a topical informative magazine with articles of interest on the construction trade.
  - This is their "worst" issue of the year because it lists only the major firms and contains no content articles. Wait for next month's issue.
  - I recommend receiving this magazine.

Direct mail/testimonials

This is the least expensive solution; it costs the marketeer the price of a stamp. Marketeer letters reflect a lack of thinking and appear to be commensurate with the stamp cost. Listed are typical quotes from real letters. Names were changed and design firm initials were alphabetized to save further embarrassment. The marketeers who wrote these letters know who they are.

> Our firm is ABC Design and we are better than DEF Architects and GHI Interiors.

These letters get tossed! Why degrade another firm? Knocking your competition does not persuade anyone to avoid the firm. In fact, the facility manager is almost challenged by ABC Design to use DEF and GHI.

A letter is a precious way of reaching your target market at 8 a.m. in the privacy of the facility manager's office. The marketeer should spend the sentences of the letter extolling the virtues of ABC Design.

> F. Manager, vice president of JK Corporation, said that LM Designers did a great job on JK's headquarters.

These are genuine reactions, and there is no doubt that the job was excellent. However, no two jobs are ever alike. The firm has to tell the facility manager what they can do for the project at hand. After all, if all jobs were the same, you could just send over the blueprints and reduce the design fees accordingly. These letters get filed in that circular file under the desk.

> The attached list of corporate references shows the quality of projects that NOP Group handles.

Facility managers always enjoy reading the list. If a firm is not attractive to facility managers, they can quickly see which corporations have already made a fatal mistake in hiring this firm. In reality, each corporation has different facilities, staff concerns, real property, standards, and budgets. It is a list that is read by the facility manager and then discarded.

> I am the principal partner of QRST Collaborative and I guarantee my personal attention on each and every project.

Here's the one person making $125 per hour or more. The partner is planning to spend the facility manager's hard-to-get funds by sitting in on all meetings. The project director and the designer are essential to the project. Let the partner attend a minimal amount of conferences and keep the fee in line.

> I am the principal of UVW Associates, formerly the partner of XYZ Design. My new firm is superior.

The facility manager has enough problems without having to deal with a new firm with no experience working as a team. Come back when you've got some work done elsewhere. Not every facility manager wants to be the "first" to use a firm or product.

> AA Design does quality work. I will be calling your secretary in a few weeks to set an appointment.

This letter gets through to the facility manager.

Brochures

These are beautiful, expensive statements reflecting a firm's work. The brochures come in a variety of very imaginative types and sizes:

Types
- Spiral-bound
- Three rings on the left side
- Two rings on the top
- Slip-out and slip-in
- Foldout
- Lift-up
- Boxed
- Die-cut

Sizes
- 5 × 8 inches
- 8 × 10 inches

- 8½ × 11 inches
- 11 × 17 inches

Delivery. These brochures are delivered to the facility manager by a number of standard methods:

- Regular mail
- Messenger
- Trade show booths
- In person
- Through a third party (an example: a realtor who has the design firms brochure for you)
- Express mail

The shape, size, and form of delivery do not matter since the insides all contain the same obligatory photos of the reception area and grand stairway.

Cold canvas calls

Marketeers must have possession of the world's most complete list of facility contacts. The day would not be complete without the facility manager's receiving calls from unknown firms.

A cold call means that there is no known project or reason for the marketeer to call, except that you are the target person who uses/employs that type of firm. The conversation usually starts with the marketeer's asking the facility manager about a rumored project. If the project exists, then the "foot is in the door." The facility manager will be subjected to a few minutes of subjective talk. If the project does not exist, then the "foot is in the mouth." The facility manager simply ends the conversation.

I suggest you request that the marketeer send the brochure (with the photos of unoccupied spaces) and a business card, and call back in several weeks.

In-person presentations

The impression of the facility manager's being overloaded with work is the reason the marketeer says, "Let's do lunch." After all, the marketeers feel that lunchtime is on the facility manager's own time. This is not the case because we are filled with anxieties about ongoing projects. Lunchtime is no different from the rest of the day.

What's wrong with breakfast at 7:30 a.m.? What's wrong with requesting a regularly scheduled meeting during the day?

When there is a "one-on-one" meeting, the marketeer must follow these rules:

- Be on time or lose your place for the month.
- Come to the point quickly by showing the product.
- Discuss the pricing.
- Leave promptly.

There is nothing worse than a marketeer who shows a great firm or product but has to check with the office prior to releasing a price or discount percentage. On second thought, there is something worse— marketeers who overstay their welcome. It is a rare visit when a marketeer gets an order on a first meeting.

Marketeers will be prepared, leave on cue, and make their commissions by spending time productively—getting on to their next call. Firms should employ marketeers on the basis of number of calls; the incentive would be there to leave quickly.

Facility managers are blessed with excellent memories for detail. The sales pitch will be remembered; no need to call the very next day to see if the facility manager has an order: "Remember me? I met you just yesterday." Oversell kills the sale every time.

Pricing.   When all is said and done, the facility manager will need to know the price of the product or firm. In some cases, marketeers will be asked to bid or submit a quote on a specific project. At other times, facility managers will want a price list or discount schedule for an upcoming project.

New firms consider an extra low price. The facility manager is well educated and knows the general price range for a particular item. So a low, low price usually is a flag to the facility manager to watch out for hidden extras, missing items, reduced quality, or some other "less-than-normal" circumstance.

Even if all criteria are met, the facility manager does not have to use the low, low firm. Why bother with the new firm at low prices and get hit with the regular pricing for the next job? Who has the time to teach the firm the workings of the corporation to save money just this one time? The facility manager will be looking for the long-term relationship.

High pricing of a firm or for a product conveys a completely different message. The initial impression is of a high-quality item or company. The next impression is that of "you get what you pay for!" You pay a high price, and you get a high invoice. There are plenty of products of high quality that are reasonably priced.

I recommend that marketeers price their product at market rate or discount a point or two. Sell us service.

Closure. Every furniture manufacturer has a "C" or "D" or "E" chair. Every design firm has planned Steelcase or Herman Miller or whatever system is utilized by the facility manager. Every raised-floor manufacturer has done rolling weight tests and has photos to show you. Every furniture dealer has installed over 100 floors of furniture this year.

Do not use any of these as evidence of firm's superiority over another firm. These criteria are all *expected* minimums. Facility managers are interested in many intangibles, such as service, delivery, knowledge of systems, assigned personnel, and general company attitude.

A talented staff combined with good pricing always wins. Personal contact appears far more advisable since each facility manager has unique problems and each company is different.

I guess Professor Harold Hill of *The Music Man* was right when he said, "You gotta know the territory." Facility professionals demand products and services tailored just enough to meet their individual corporate needs. It is not that difficult for marketeers to take a few moments to tailor-make their pitch to meet the needs of every potential client.

9.3 An Open Letter to Marketeers

Dear Marketeers:

Do yourself and the facility manager a favor before you call, write that letter, lick the envelope, start videotaping, fold the brochure, or build the booth: Do your homework. Learn the customer's needs.

Facility managers need you to update them on your firm's or product's availability, innovation, and cost. You need the facility manager to update you on current market demands and the future market needs as well.

Remember, think ahead.

When you, the marketeer, respect the facility manager's rights and time, you will receive this respect back in terms of orders that will become future studies in the next edition of "Marketing 101."

Cordially,

Facility Manager

9.4 Questions and Answers for the Marketeers

Questions marketeers wanted to ask facility managers but were afraid to hear the answers for:

Question 1. Do facility managers want to hear from another design firm or about another new product?

Answer 1a. Yes. Facility managers use anywhere from 2 to 20 different design firms at the same time and at least 150 different vendors for furnishings. Firms and products burn out, top people move on, prices seem to rise each year. Facility managers need fresh ideas, fresh firms, new colors, new items, and new approaches to old problems.

Answer 1b. No. Facility managers do not want to train new firms on space standards, methodologies, rules, and staff. After all, facility managers don't have the time. Facility managers do not want to be the testing ground for new design firms that started last month, or for established firms that have all new management. Facility managers do not want to see new, secret furniture systems stored in a warehouse in Michigan. The reason is simple. The secret system is handmade, one of a kind, and not available for 9 months. Furthermore, most vendors require facility managers to sign a release forbidding them to reveal what they saw or where they saw it.

Question 2. Should the marketeer take the facility manager to lunch?

Answer 2a. Yes. Marketeers feel it's essential to get you out of your environment. It is a chance to be alone without the telephone constantly ringing. It is their chance to discuss that tailor-made pitch without the pressures of the office. These are valid reasons.

Answer 2b. No. Facility managers do not want to be under any obligations or influences brought about by the so-called free lunch. Facility managers out to breakfast or lunch will miss a half dozen "do-or-die" telephone calls. A 2-hour lunch eats away inside the facility manager more than the food consumed. Facility managers have projects to follow up on, deliveries to check, and construction to supervise.

Facility managers carefully plan for the fourth dimension. But time is *not* on the facility manager's side.

Question 3. How good is the facility manager's memory?

Answer 3a. Excellent. Facility managers remember virtually all details about every project, over longer periods—only significant details—every complaint and every compliment, every unique happening and unusual event, every humorous project story, every mistake and every success, every product specified which came late or damaged, and every vendor's cocktail party. *Answer 3b.* Terrible. Facility managers cannot remember *your name, firm, or product* when seeking three bidders.

Question 4. How organized is the facility manager?
Answer 4a. Very. Facility managers can find any file folder within 5 minutes, find the memorandum the boss wants within another 2 minutes, and list the sequences, in order, of every step left to complete on any number of open projects.
Answer 4b. Not very. Facility managers cannot find the marketeer's brochure or catalog, recall receiving the marketeer's letter, locate the marketeer's business card.

Marketeers should bring along another copy.

9.5   The Words of Others—Marketing Savvy

Anne Fallucchi   *Editor and Copublisher,*
Facilities Design & Management

For a field with big-dollar clout, facilities management was all but ignored as recently as a decade ago. Today, it's a different story.

Marketing-savvy manufacturers have targeted the facilities manager as a strong and important customer. Seem obvious? Yet only a handful of years ago, manufacturers were protective of their bread-and-butter A & D community, as they label interior designers and architects designing for their corporate clients. In fact, it wasn't too far back when manufacturer showrooms locked their doors to the end user unless the designer was present, with the facilities manager following three steps behind.

Marketing-savvy interior design and architecture firms now list "facilities management" on their roster of services. An interesting strategic move for many, given their earlier plaint that the facilities manager represented, in their minds, loss of business. Now the opposite has proved true. Those who early recognized this new business potential are reaping profitable benefits with their expanded services.

Marketing-savvy marts, design centers, and independent groups are pulling out all stops to entice facilities managers to their annual contract (commercial/institutional) market days and conference/exhibitions. The first to give official recognition, Chicago's Merchandise Mart, in 1982 labeled one of its four NEOCON days as Facilities Day.

The New York market organization, Designer's Saturday, followed suit later that year with its designated Facilities Management Day, complete with facilities-oriented showroom seminars and keynote speaker. Independent conference/exhibitions are more and more frequently addressing the corporate facilities manager: Workspace; MIT's Office of Facilities Management Conference; Canadian Facility Management Show and Conference. There are many others and probably more to come in the near future.

Marketing-savvy colleges and universities, having recognized a new student body, are developing special facilities management courses and even full programs. Three are currently offering facilities management graduate degree programs: Cornell University pioneered the first degree program in 1980, Grand Valley State College did so in 1982, and 1987 saw Michigan State announce its own.

Marketing-savvy facilities managers—you among them, since you are reading this book—have by your work fostered a greater understanding within the corporate structure on the importance of facilities, asset, and people-oriented management. But only 10 years ago, the label "facilities manager" rarely if at all appeared as a corporate title. Today it abounds, often with the designation "vice president" leading it off.

Let's not forget IFMA—International Facility Management Association. Starting in 1979 with a mere handful of interested (and frustrated, they tell me) practitioners, the Houston-based professional organization now numbers more than 5000 members, one proof of its need, its success, its ongoing growth. Further proof: The 1987 annual IFMA conference more than doubled attendance over the prior year. Among IFMA's many other activities are specialized research programs to give members valuable information to help elevate the facilities management process within their corporations. Yes, IFMA even offers a job information service.

When *Facilities Design & Management* was launched in 1982 expressly for facilities management practioners, we editors identified facilities management as an "emerging" profession. Clearly, it's no longer true, for facilities management has since shed its fledgling cocoon. It's fully grown and maturing beautifully.

Index

About the Author

Stephen Binder is Vice President of Facilities Planning and Director of Project Management in the Real Property Services Division of Citibank, N.A. In this capacity he is responsible for executive management of 60 office sites with more than 9.2 million rentable square feet. He received the International Facility Management Association's Distinguished Member Award in 1987 and has served on IFMA's Board of Directors as Treasurer and as the Northeast Regional Vice President. Mr. Binder resides in Port Washington, New York.